Finite-State Text Processing

Synthesis Lectures on Human Language Technologies

Editor
Graeme Hirst, *University of Toronto*

Synthesis Lectures on Human Language Technologies is edited by Graeme Hirst of the University of Toronto. The series consists of 50- to 150-page monographs on topics relating to natural language processing, computational linguistics, information retrieval, and spoken language understanding. Emphasis is on important new techniques, on new applications, and on topics that combine two or more HLT subfields.

Finite-State Text Processing
Kyle Gorman and Richard Sproat
2021

Embeddings in Natural Language Processing: Theory and Advances in Vector Representations of Meaning
Mohammad Taher Pilehvar and Jose Camacho-Collados
2020

Conversational AI: Dialogue Systems, Conversational Agents, and Chatbots
Michael McTear
2020

Natural Language Processing for Social Media, Third Edition
Anna Atefeh Farzindar and Diana Inkpen
2020

Statistical Significance Testing for Natural Language Processing
Rotem Dror, Lotem Peled, Segev Shlomov, and Roi Reichart
2020

Deep Learning Approaches to Text Production
Shashi Narayan and Claire Gardent
2020

Linguistic Fundamentals for Natural Language Processing II: 100 Essentials from
Semantics and Pragmatics
Emily M. Bender and Alex Lascarides
2019

Cross-Lingual Word Embeddings
Anders Søgaard, Ivan Vulić, Sebastian Ruder, Manaal Faruqui
2019

Bayesian Analysis in Natural Language Processing, Second Edition
Shay Cohen
2019

Argumentation Mining
Manfred Stede and Jodi Schneider
2018

Quality Estimation for Machine Translation
Lucia Specia, Carolina Scarton, and Gustavo Henrique Paetzold
2018

Natural Language Processing for Social Media, Second Edition
Atefeh Farzindar and Diana Inkpen
2017

Automatic Text Simplification
Horacio Saggion
2017

Neural Network Methods for Natural Language Processing
Yoav Goldberg
2017

Syntax-based Statistical Machine Translation
Philip Williams, Rico Sennrich, Matt Post, and Philipp Koehn
2016

Domain-Sensitive Temporal Tagging
Jannik Strötgen and Michael Gertz
2016

Linked Lexical Knowledge Bases: Foundations and Applications
Iryna Gurevych, Judith Eckle-Kohler, and Michael Matuschek
2016

Bayesian Analysis in Natural Language Processing
Shay Cohen
2016

Finite-State Text Processing

Kyle Gorman and Richard Sproat

ISBN: 978-3-031-01051-4   paperback
ISBN: 978-3-031-02179-4   ebook
ISBN: 978-3-031-00190-1   hardcover

DOI 10.1007/978-3-031-02179-4

A Publication in the Springer series
SYNTHESIS LECTURES ON HUMAN LANGUAGE TECHNOLOGIES

Lecture #50
Series Editor: Graeme Hirst, *University of Toronto*
Series ISSN
Print 1947-4040   Electronic 1947-4059

Finite-State Text Processing

Kyle Gorman
Graduate Center, City University of New York

Richard Sproat
Google LLC

SYNTHESIS LECTURES ON HUMAN LANGUAGE TECHNOLOGIES #50

ABSTRACT

Weighted finite-state transducers (WFSTs) are commonly used by engineers and computational linguists for processing and generating speech and text. This book first provides a detailed introduction to this formalism. It then introduces Pynini, a Python library for compiling finite-state grammars and for combining, optimizing, applying, and searching finite-state transducers. This book illustrates this library's conventions and use with a series of case studies. These include the compilation and application of context-dependent rewrite rules, the construction of morphological analyzers and generators, and text generation and processing applications.

KEYWORDS

automata, finite automata, finite-state automata, finite-state transducers, grammar development, language processing, speech processing, state machines, text generation, text processing, Python, Pynini

Contents

Preface

This book is our attempt to provide a "one-stop" reference for engineers and linguists interested in using finite-state technologies for text generation and processing. As such, it begins with formal language and automata theory, topics covered in much greater detail by textbooks such as Hopcroft et al. 2008 and handbook chapters such as Mohri 2009. In our experience, full command of finite-state technologies requires familiarity with a number of matters that have not received much attention in prior literature. Among these topics is the theory of semirings, and algorithms specific to weighted automata such as the shortest-distance and shortest-path algorithms. These formalisms and algorithms are key for finite-state speech recognition. Furthermore, there exist many text processing applications that resemble weighted finite-state-based speech recognition insofar as hypotheses—that is, possible output strings—are represented as paths through a lattice constructed via composition of weighted automata, and inference/decoding involves computing the shortest path.

Users interested in text applications also stand to benefit from lesser-known "tricks of the trade" for finite-state development. These tricks include fuzzy string matching (Figure 7.1), efficient algorithms for optimizing arbitrary weighted finite-state transducers (section 4.1), compiling rewrite rules (section 5.2) and morphological analyzers and generators (chapter 6), and applying these transducers to sets of strings (section 5.3).

At the same time, we wish to go beyond algebraic formalisms and pseudocode. Thus, we illustrate our examples with Pynini, an open-source Python library for weighted finite-state transducers developed at Google. Still, we are skeptical that anything made out of dead trees is an appropriate medium for documenting a rapidly changing software library. So whereas earlier texts like *Finite State Morphology* (Beesley and Karttunen 2003) are in some sense *about* the Xerox finite-state toolkit as it existed at the time, we hope that this is not merely a book about Pynini. It is our hope that this melange of formalisms and algorithms, code and applications, meets the needs of our readers.

Finally, in the current age we would be remiss if we did not stress the importance of ethical use of this—or indeed any—technology. Ten years ago, Sproat (2010a:255) pointed out the potential dangers for society of language technology and its misuse, especially on social media platforms, noting that "language can be abused, and so can the technology that supports it". The recent rise in disinformation on social media has unfortunately made those concerns seem all too prophetic. The ongoing pandemic, aggravated in large part by disinformation, has brought these dangers into even starker relief. It is therefore our profound hope that the technology described in this book only be used for the betterment of humankind. One example of this sort suggests itself: Markov et al. (2021) describe how regular expression matching is used to determine whether a post on social media mentions COVID-19 so it can be screened for disinformation.

Kyle Gorman and Richard Sproat
April 2021

Acknowledgments

We first owe an enormous debt to the many Google engineers who have contributed over the years to the OpenFst and OpenGrm libraries, particularly Cyril Allauzen, Brian Roark, Michael Riley, and Jeffrey Sorensen. Substantial improvements to the Pynini library have been made by Lawrence Wolf-Sonkin, and this book has greatly benefited from the user community of Google linguists, especially Sandy Ritchie. Thanks to Anssi Yli-Jyrä and an anonymous reviewer for their detailed reviews; to Jeffrey Heinz for detailed feedback on our pre-final draft; to Alëna Aksënova, Hossep Dolatian, Jordan Kodner, Constantine Lignos, Fred Mailhot, and Arya McCarthy, who provided useful comments on early drafts of the book; and to Chandan Narayan for notes on Pāṇini.

Kyle Gorman and Richard Sproat
April 2021

CHAPTER 1

Finite-State Machines

This is a book about **weighted finite-state transducers** (WFSTs) and their use in text generation and processing. The WFST formalism synthesizes decades of research into graphs, automata, and formal languages, including lines of research blossoming long before the era of ubiquitous digital computing.

The history of finite-state technology stretches back almost a century. Some key theorems and algorithms were discovered—and rediscovered—long before computers became powerful enough to exploit them (see chapter 5 for an example) and in some cases decades have elapsed between discovery and software implementation. Some essential algorithms were not generalized until the 1990s or later, as part of efforts—particularly at AT&T Bell Labs, and later at Google—to use WFSTs for scalable automatic speech recognition and text-to-speech synthesis.

A few key notions connect these disparate areas of research and application. The first is that of the **state machine**, a sort of abstract mathematical model of computation of which weighted finite-state transducers are a special case. Such models, first formalized by Turing (1936), are not only the foundation of the theory of computation—quite literally, the study of what it means to compute—but also inspired the creation of ENIAC, the first general-purpose digital computer, a decade later. The second is that of **formal languages**. While the origins of formal language theory can be traced at least as far back as Thue (1914), perhaps the most important contribution is a study by Kleene (1956) first circulated in 1951. Kleene's study springs from an obscure goal: the formal characterization of the expressive capacity of "nerve nets", a primitive form of artificial neural network proposed by McCulloch and Pitts (1943) a few years prior. To do so, Kleene introduces a family of formal languages called the "regular languages" and established strong connections between the algebraic characterizations of formal language theory and the automata (i.e., state machine) characterizations used by Turing and others. This body of work was an enormous inspiration in the development of modern linguistic theory—generative grammar in particular (Chomsky 1963)—and also contributed to the theory of compilers, computer programs which translate other computer programs. This chapter traces these two threads—automata and formal languages—and their relationship.

All of this effort, by some of the greatest scientific minds of the early 20th century, could easily have come to naught had the objects of study—regular languages and finite-state automata—turned out to have limited real-world relevance. But it turns out that these exhibit tantalizing similarities to phenomena found in natural—that is, human—languages, a fact which has only become clearer with time. A few examples should suffice. It is now believed that virtually all patterns that define the phonology—or the grapheme-to-phoneme rules—of natural languages can be expressed as relations between regular languages. The hypothesis space of automatic speech recognizers, consisting of a probabilistic mapping between acoustic observations and word sequences, can also be compactly expressed as a relation between two regular languages. Finally, many text generation and processing problems can be framed as transductions between regular languages. Thanks to Kleene and others, it is known that these types of relations can be encoded by state machines, and subsequent work introduces techniques for combining, applying, optimizing, and searching these machines.

1.1   STATE MACHINES

A **state machine** is hardware or software whose behavior can be described solely in terms of a set of **states** and **arcs**, which represent transitions between those states. In this formalism, states roughly correspond to "memory" and arcs to "operations" or "computations". State machines are examples of what computer scientists call **directed graphs**.[1] These are "directed" in the sense that the existence of an arc from state q to state r does not imply an arc from r to q. A **finite-state machine** is merely a state machine with a finite, predetermined set of states and labeled arcs.

One familiar example of a state machine—encoded in hardware, rather than software—is the old-fashioned gumball machine (Figure 1.1). Such machines can be in exactly one of two states at a time, and each state is associated with actions such as

- turning the knob,

- inserting a coin, or

- emitting a gumball.

At one state, arbitrarily called state 0, it is possible to turn the knob, but this has no effect on the behavior of the machine. If, on the other hand, one inserts the appropriate coin(s), that transitions the machine to a state 1, at which point a subsequent turn of the knob will cause the machine to emit a gumball and return to state 0. This of course is an idealization of real-world gumball machines, which may experience mechanical failure or run out of gumballs. Without a shop-keeper around to service the machine, model and reality necessarily diverge.

The description of the gumball machine above is given a graphical representation in Figure 1.2. By convention, the bold outline of state 0 indicates that it has been—arbitrarily—chosen as the **start** or **initial state**; the double-struck outline indicates that it is also a **final state**; these notions will be formalized shortly. Valid transitions between states are indicated with arrows. These arcs are labeled with pairs of actions. Here, the inputs are user actions and the outputs are gumballs. The Greek letter ϵ ("epsilon") is used to represent the absence of an input and/or

---

[1]The primary difference is terminological; what are here called **states** and **arcs** are known in other communities as "vertices" and "edges", respectively.

Figure 1.1: An old-fashioned gumball machine. (Image credit: Dario Lo Presti/Shutterstock. com)

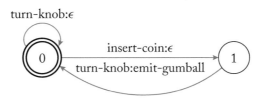

Figure 1.2: An old-fashioned gumball machine schematized as a state machine.

output for a given arc. Because, as mentioned, turning the knob at state 0 produces no output and does not change the state of the machine, there is a self-arc at state 0 labeled turn-knob:ϵ. On the other hand, inserting a coin at state 0 produces no observable output, but it transitions the machine to state 1. At this state a knob turn by the user causes the machine to emit a gumball and return to state 0.

We now provide definitions for various types of finite-state machine, after reviewing some formal preliminaries.

1.2   FORMAL PRELIMINARIES

This section provides a brief introduction to set theory and related topics. Those readers already familiar with sets, relations, functions, strings, and languages are welcome to skip to section 1.3.

1.2.1   SETS

Sets are abstract, unordered collections of distinct objects. They are an abstract, purely logical notion, and their definition does not presuppose any particular method of representing them in hardware or software; they are unordered in the sense that there is no natural ordering among the **elements** or **members** of any set. By convention, sets are represented using uppercase Greek or Italic letters, and elements of sets are denoted using lowercase Italic letters. Set membership is indicated using the $\in$ symbol, e.g., $x \in X$ is read "x is a member of X". Non-membership is written using the $\notin$ symbol, e.g., $x \notin X$ is read "x is not a member of X".

Members of a set can be any type of object, including other sets. There are several ways to specify the members of a set. First, for finite sets, one can simply list the elements in the set enclosed in curly braces, a representation called **extensional** or **list notation**. For instance, $\{2, 3, 5, 7\}$ is the finite set of prime numbers less than 10. An alternative notation, and the only one which can be used to denote infinite sets, uses a predicate such that if some element satisfies the predicate, that element is a member of a set; this is known as **intensional**, **predicate**, **set-builder**, or **set-former** notation. For instance, one might indicate the infinite set of prime numbers using the notation $\{x \mid \text{prime}(x)\}$. Finally, special notation is used for the **empty set**, the set with no elements: it is written $\emptyset$. The **cardinality** of a set X, written $|X|$, is the number of distinct elements in the set.

A set X is said to be a **subset** of another set Y if every element in X is also a member of Y. This property is written using the $\subseteq$ operator, e.g., $X \subseteq Y$ is read "X is a subset of Y". X is a **proper subset** of Y ($X \subset Y$) if and only if X is a subset of Y and $X \neq Y$.

There are various logical operations over sets. Given two sets X and Y, their **intersection** $X \cap Y$ is the set that contains all elements which are members of both X and Y: that is, $X \cap Y = \{z \mid z \in X \wedge z \in Y\}$ where $\wedge$ represents logical AND. Given two sets X and Y, their **union** $X \cup Y$ is the set that contains all elements which are members of X, Y, or both: that is, $X \cup Y = \{z \mid z \in X \vee z \in Y\}$ where $\vee$ represents logical OR. Finally, their **difference** $X - Y$ is the set that contains all elements which are members of X but not of Y: that is, $X - Y = \{z \mid z \in X \wedge z \notin Y\}$.

1.2.2   RELATIONS AND FUNCTIONS

A **pair** or **two-tuple** is a sequence of two elements, e.g., (a, b) is the pair consisting of a then b. This is used to define an operation over sets known as the **cross-product** or **Cartesian product**. Given two sets X and Y, their cross-product $X \times Y$ is the set containing all ordered pairs (x, y) where x is an element of X and Y is an element of Y. That is, $X \times Y = \{(x, y) \mid x \in X \land y \in Y\}$.

A **relation**—specifically, a **binary** or **two-way relation**—over sets X and Y is a subset of the cross-product $X \times Y$. In this book, relations are indicated using lowercase Greek letters, and the **domain**—set of inputs—and **range** (or more properly, the **codomain**)—the set of outputs— are usually provided upon first definition. For instance, the expression $\gamma \subseteq X \times Y$ indicate that γ is a relation with domain X and range Y. Relations represent mappings between elements of the domain and elements of the range; for instance, the "less than" relation can be written $\lambda \subseteq \mathbb{R} \times \mathbb{R} = \{(x, y) \mid x < y\}$ where $\mathbb{R}$ is the set of real numbers.

A **function** is a relation for which every element of the domain is associated with exactly one element of the range. The "less than" relation above is not a function because, for example, there are an infinitude of real numbers that are less than any other real number. However, the "successor" relation $\sigma \subseteq \mathbb{N} \times \mathbb{N} = \{(x, x + 1) \mid x \in \mathbb{N}\}$, where $\mathbb{N}$ is the set of natural numbers, is a function, because each natural number has exactly one successor.

Three-, four-, and five-way relations, and so on, are all well-defined, though there is no such generalization for functions, since n-way relations where $n > 2$ lack well-defined domain and range. However, one can redefine any n-way relation into a two-way relation by grouping the various sets into domain and range; for instance, a four-way relation over $A \times B \times C \times D$ can be redefined as a two-way relation (and possibly, a function) with domain $A \times B$ and range $C \times D$. Such a relation might be defined as a subset of $A \times B \to C \times D$, with the arrow used to indicate the partition into domain and range.

The application of an input argument to a relation or function can be indicated using square brackets. For instance, given the successor function σ, then $\sigma[3] = \{4\}$ because $(3, 4) \in \sigma$.

Given a relation $\gamma \subseteq X \times Y$ and $x \in X$, $\gamma[x] \downarrow$ indicates that γ is well defined at x and $\gamma[x] \uparrow$ indicates that γ is undefined at x. A relation or function is said to be **total** if it is defined for all values of the domain. The less-than relation and successor functions, for example, are both total.

1.2.3   STRINGS AND LANGUAGES

Many of the sets defined below contain a type of element known as a string. Let Σ be a set of symbols called the **alphabet**. A **string** is a finite ordered sequence of zero or more elements from the alphabet. By convention, the empty string is indicated by ϵ. Note that ϵ is not a member of Σ.

The **concatenation** of two strings is the string produced by joining the two strings end-to-end. The concatenation of two strings x, y is written xy. Note that ϵ is the concatenative identity, thus $x\epsilon = \epsilon x = x$ for all x.

A set of zero or more strings is known as a **language**.[2] Since languages are sets, operations such as intersection, union, and difference are well defined. In addition, concatenation can also be generalized to languages, i.e., given languages X and Y, $XY = \{xy \mid x \in X \wedge y \in Y\}$. One other operation over languages is closure. First, the notation X^n, where n is a natural number, denotes a language consisting of n self-concatenations of X; e.g., $X^0 = \{\epsilon\}$ and $X^4 = XXXX$. The (**concatenative**) **closure** of a language X is an infinite union of zero or more concatenations of X with itself. It is notated with a superscripted asterisk, e.g., $X^* = \bigcup_{i \geq 0} X^i = \{\epsilon\} \cup X \cup XX \cup XXX \cup \ldots$. One variant of closure, indicated with a superscript plus-sign, excludes the empty string, e.g., $X^+ = \bigcup_{i > 0} X^i = X \cup XX \cup XXX \cup \ldots$, or equivalently, $X^+ = XX^*$. These two variants of closure are sometimes referred to as **Kleene star** and **Kleene plus**, respectively. Finally, a superscripted question mark is used to indicate optionality, e.g., $X^? = \{\epsilon\} \cup X$.

1.3   ACCEPTORS AND REGULAR LANGUAGES

Finite acceptors are the simplest form of finite automata, in some ways simpler than the model of a gumball machine presented above. They represent a family of string sets known as the regular languages.

1.3.1   FINITE-STATE ACCEPTORS

A **finite-state acceptor** (FSA) is a five-tuple consisting of

1. a finite set of states Q,

2. a **start** or **initial state** $s \in Q$,

3. a set of **final** (or **accepting**) **states** $F \subseteq Q$,

4. an **alphabet** Σ, and

5. a **transition relation** $\delta \subseteq Q \times (\Sigma \cup \{\epsilon\}) \times Q$.

Note that as formalized here, there is only one start state but there may be many final states; also note that the start state may itself be a final state.[3]

An FSA is said to accept a string if there exists a path from the initial state to some final state, and the labels of the arcs traversed by that path correspond to the string in question. The set of all strings so accepted by an FSA is called its language. More formally, given two states $q, r \in Q$ and a symbol $z \in \Sigma \cup \{\epsilon\}$, $(q, z, r) \in \delta$ implies that there is an arc from state q to state r with label z. A **path** through a finite acceptor is a pair of

---

[2]This is not intended to supplant common-sense notions of what a language is; it is merely a term of art.

[3]One could allow for arbitrarily many start states, but given any finite automaton with multiple start states $S \subseteq Q$, it is trivial to construct an equivalent automaton with a single "superinitial" start state. Alternatively, one could limit the formalism to a single "superfinal" final state $f \in Q$.

1. a state sequence $q_1, q_2, \ldots, q_n \in Q^n$ and a

2. a string $z_1, z_2, \ldots, z_n \in (\Sigma \cup \{\epsilon\})^n$,

subject to the constraint that $\forall i \in [1, n] : (q_i, z_i, q_{i+1}) \in \delta$; that is, there exists an arc from q_i to q_{i+1} labeled z_i. A path that visits a state more than one time—i.e., if its state sequence contains the start state s or any repeated states—has a **cycle**. Automata are **cyclic** if any of their paths contain cycles and **acyclic** otherwise.

A path is said to be **complete** if

1. $(s, z_1, q_1) \in \delta$ and

2. $q_n \in F$.

That is, a complete path must also begin with an arc from the initial state s to q_1 labeled z_1 and terminate at a final state. Henceforth, without loss of generality, ϵ-labels are omitted from path strings because ϵ signals the absence of a symbol and therefore can be ignored. Indeed, for every FSA, there is an equivalent ϵ-**free** FSA, i.e., an FSA which accepts the same language but which has no ϵ-arcs, computed with the ϵ-removal algorithm (Mohri 2002a). Then, an FSA **accepts** or **recognizes** a string $z \in \Sigma^*$ if there exists a complete path with string z. The set of strings accepted by an FSA is called its language.

1.3.2   REGULAR LANGUAGES

The family of languages recognized by finite acceptors are the **regular languages**. Kleene (1956) provides an algebraic characterization. Given an alphabet Σ:

1. The empty language $\emptyset$ is a regular language.

2. The empty string language $\{\epsilon\}$ is a regular language.

3. If $s \in \Sigma$, then the singleton language $\{s\}$ is a regular language.

4. If X is a regular language, then its closure X^* is a regular language.

5. If X, Y are regular languages, then:

   - their concatenation XY is a regular language, and
   - their union $X \cup Y$ is a regular language.

6. Languages which cannot be derived as above are not regular languages.

Kleene (ibid.) also shows that every finite acceptor corresponds to a regular language and that every regular language corresponds to a finite acceptor. This result, known as **Kleene's theorem**, implies that operations over languages such as closure, concatenation, and union are defined not only for languages but also for finite acceptors.

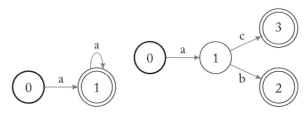

Figure 1.3: Finite acceptors for the languages $\{a\}^+$ (left) and $\{a\}(\{b\} \cup \{c\})$ (right).

Two examples of FSAs and their corresponding regular languages are shown in Figure 1.3 as **state transition diagrams**. The left pane contains an FSA defined by $Q = \{0, 1\}$, $s = 0$, $F = \{1\}$, $\Sigma = \{a\}$, and $\delta = \{(0, a, 1), (1, a, 1)\}$, which accepts the infinite language $\{a\}^+ = \{a, aa, aaa, \dots\}$. The right pane shows an FSA which accepts the finite language $\{a\}(\{b\} \cup \{c\}) = \{ab, ac\}$. The reader is encouraged to study these acceptors and manually trace the generation of a few strings.

1.3.3 REGULAR EXPRESSIONS

Regular expressions are a declarative notational scheme used to characterize the regular languages (Hopcroft et al. 2008: ch. 3). One can convert any finite acceptor to a regular expression, and any regular expression to a finite automaton. However, implementations of regular expressions in many programming languages—for instance, the implementation used in Python's built-in re module—include additional features which cannot be encoded using regular languages or finite-state acceptors.

1.4 TRANSDUCERS AND RATIONAL RELATIONS

Finite transducers are a generalization of finite acceptors. Rather than modeling languages, they model **rational relations** between pairs of languages, and as such they can be used to encode string-to-string transductions.[4]

1.4.1 FINITE-STATE TRANSDUCERS

A **finite-state transducer** (FST) is a six-tuple consisting of

1. a finite set of states Q,

2. a start state $s \in Q$,

3. a set of final states $F \subseteq Q$,

---

[4]It is possible to generalize rational relations, and finite-state transducers, to relations between sets of more than two languages. This generalization is not discussed here as it is only rarely employed in computational linguistics, but see, e.g., Kay 1987, Kiraz 2001, or Hulden 2017.

4. an **input alphabet** Σ,

5. an **output alphabet** Φ, and

6. a transition relation $\delta \subseteq Q \times (\Sigma \cup \{\epsilon\}) \times (\Phi \cup \{\epsilon\}) \times Q$.

The first three elements are also used in the definition of FSAs; the latter three are novel. The key distinction between FSAs and FSTs is that in the latter case, arcs bear pairs of labels, one drawn from an input alphabet and the other from a (possibly disjoint) output alphabet. A **path** through a finite transducer is a triple consisting of

1. a state sequence $q_1, q_2, \ldots, q_n \in Q^n$,

2. an input string $x_1, x_2, \ldots, x_n \in (\Sigma \cup \{\epsilon\})^n$, and

3. an output string $y_1, y_2, \ldots, y_n \in (\Phi \cup \{\epsilon\})^n$,

subject to the constraint that $\forall i \in [1, n] : (q_i, x_i, y_i, q_{i+1}) \in \delta$. A **complete path** is a path where

1. $(s, x_1, y_1, q_1) \in \delta$ and

2. $q_n \in F$.

That is, a complete path must also begin with a transition from the initial state s to q_i with input label x_i and output label y_i and halt in a final state. Without loss of generality, and once again ignoring the presence of ϵ, the domain Σ^* and range Φ^* of an FST are both themselves regular languages, and the FST itself can be interpreted as a relation, a subset of the cross-product $\Sigma^* \times \Phi^*$. Then, an FST **transduces** or **maps** from $x \in \Sigma^*$ to $y \in \Phi^*$ so long as a complete path with input string x and output string y exists. However, unlike FSAs, not all FSTs have an equivalent ϵ-free form. For example, consider an FST mapping from two-character U.S. state abbreviations (e.g., OH) to state names (Ohio); a fragment of such an FST is shown in Figure 1.4. Here, arcs with ϵ input labels are necessary to allow input strings which are shorter than the corresponding output strings. Note also that the ϵ-removal algorithm mentioned in subsection 1.3.1 removes ϵ-arcs—those which have ϵ as both input and output labels—not ϵ-labels in general.

1.4.2   RATIONAL RELATIONS

The family of string relations that can be encoded as a finite-state transducer are the **rational relations**. Like regular languages, closure, concatenation, and union are all well defined for rational relations. The rational relations are closed under these operations, meaning that the closure of a rational relation, or the concatenation or union of two or more rational relations, are also rational relations. However, there are other operations, such as difference, under which the regular languages are closed but the rational relations are not.

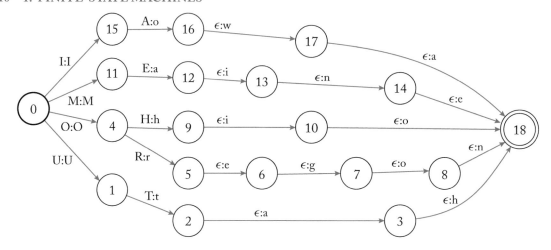

Figure 1.4: Fragment of a FST mapping from state abbreviations to state names.

Rational relations are closely related to, but distinct from, **regular expression substitutions** (e.g., as performed by Python's re.sub function).[5] On one dimension, regular expression substitutions are less expressive than rational relations, because the former permit many-to-many (rather than merely one-to-one and many-to-one) transductions, whereas the pattern matched by a re.sub is an arbitrary regular language, the substitution must be a single string. Neither finite state transducers nor the rational relations are restricted in this fashion. At the same time, re.sub implements other mechanisms that make it more expressive than rational relations.

1.5   WEIGHTED ACCEPTORS AND LANGUAGES

The above formalisms also permit an extension in which acceptors and transducers—and languages and relations—are generalized by attaching weights to states and arcs. These weights can represent virtually any set so long as the set and associated operations obey certain constraints decribed below. **Language models**, probability distributions over strings, can be compactly encoded as weighted acceptors (e.g., Allauzen et al. 2003, 2005, Roark et al. 2012); **hidden Markov models** can be encoded as weighted transducers (Roche and Schabes 1995) as can sequential **linear models** (Wu et al. 2014) and decoder graphs for automatic speech recognition engines (e.g., Mohri 1997, Mohri et al. 2002). Below, semirings are defined and exemplified and then used to generalize earlier definitions of automata, languages, and relations.

1.5.1   MONOIDS AND SEMIRINGS

Weighted automata algorithms are defined with respect to an algebraic system known as a semiring (Kuich and Salomaa 1986). It is first necessary to define a related notion, monoids.

---

[5]https://docs.python.org/3/library/re.html#re.sub

A **monoid** is an ordered pair $(\mathbb{K}, \bullet)$ where $\mathbb{K}$ is a set and $\bullet$ is a binary operator over $\mathbb{K}$ with the properties of

1. **closure**: $\forall a, b \in \mathbb{K} : a \bullet b \in \mathbb{K}$,

2. **associativity**: $\forall a, b, c \in \mathbb{K} : (a \bullet b) \bullet c = a \bullet (b \bullet c)$, and

3. **identity**: $\exists e \in \mathbb{K} : e \bullet a = a \bullet e = a$.

A monoid is said to be **commutative** if $\forall a, b \in \mathbb{K} : a \bullet b = b \bullet a$. Then, a **semiring** is then a five-tuple $(\mathbb{K}, \oplus, \otimes, \bar{0}, \bar{1})$ such that

1. the pair $(\mathbb{K}, \oplus)$ form a commutative monoid with identity element $\bar{0}$,

2. the pair $(\mathbb{K}, \otimes)$ form a monoid with identity element $\bar{1}$,

3. $\forall a, b, c \in \mathbb{K} : a \otimes (b \oplus c) = (a \otimes b) \oplus (a \otimes c)$, and

4. $\forall a \in \mathbb{K} : a \otimes \bar{0} = \bar{0} \otimes a = \bar{0}$.

These constraints require that $\oplus$ is commutative, that $\bar{0}$ is the additive identity, that $\bar{1}$ is the multiplicative identity, that $\otimes$ distributes over $\oplus$, and that $\bar{0}$ is the multiplicative annihilator (i.e., that any weight multiplied with $\bar{0}$ is $\bar{0}$). Some common semirings are shown in Table 1.1. The **Boolean semiring** consists of true (1) and false (0) values and logical OR and AND operators. The **probability semiring** ranges over positive real numbers $\mathbb{R}_+$ and employs the expected $+$ and $\times$ arithmetic operations for $\oplus$ and $\otimes$.[6] The **log semiring** is the projection of the probability semiring onto the log domain.[7] The log semiring uses the logarithmic identity $\ln(xy) = \ln x + \ln y$ to replace multiplication with addition in the log domain; this helps to avoid arithmetic underflow when weight computations are performed with floating-point numbers. The definition of addition in this semiring is somewhat more complex: $\oplus = \oplus_{\log}$ where $a \oplus_{\log} b = -\ln(e^{-a} + e^{-b})$. Finally, the **tropical semiring** is identical to the log semiring except that $\oplus = \min$.[8]

A semiring is said to exhibit the **path property** (or to be a **path semiring**) if for all $a, b \in \mathbb{K} : a \oplus b \in \{a, b\}$. The tropical semiring has this property—the minimum of any two numbers must be one of those two numbers—as does the Boolean semiring. Non-path semirings such as the probability semiring and log semirings define $\oplus$ in a way consistent with common-sense arithmetic notions, making them suitable for applications that involve counting. One example of this is the expectation maximization algorithm, commonly used to learn free parameters of speech models. In contrast, path semirings are used for decoding because the path property is required to efficiently compute the shortest path(s) through weighted automata (section 4.3).

---

[6]For probabilities, only numbers between 0 and 1 inclusive make sense, but numbers in the range $(1, +\infty]$ serve as inverse elements.

[7]The OpenFst library uses the natural logarithm, specifically.

[8]The tropical semiring is named in tribute to the late mathematician Imre Simon of the University of São Paulo. We note that São Paulo is just south of the Tropic of Capricorn, so "subtropical" would have been more apt.

Table 1.1: Some commonly used semirings for finite-state applications; $\mathbb{R}$ and $\mathbb{R}_+$ denote the real, and positive real, numbers, respectively.

	$\mathbb{K}$	$\oplus$	$\otimes$	$\bar{0}$	$\bar{1}$
Boolean	$\{0, 1\}$	$\vee$	$\wedge$	0	1
Probability	$\mathbb{R}_+$	$+$	$\times$	0	1
Log	$\mathbb{R} \cup \{\pm\infty\}$	$\oplus_{\log}$	$+$	$+\infty$	0
Tropical	$\mathbb{R} \cup \{\pm\infty\}$	$\min$	$+$	$+\infty$	0

1.5.2   WEIGHTED FINITE ACCEPTORS

A **weighted finite-state acceptor** (WFSA) is an FSA in which weights are associated with arcs and states. It is defined by a six-tuple consisting of

1. a finite set of states Q,

2. a start state $s \in Q$,

3. a **semiring** $(\mathbb{K}, \oplus, \otimes, \bar{0}, \bar{1})$,

4. a **final weight function** $\omega \subseteq Q \times \mathbb{K}$,

5. an alphabet Σ, and

6. a **transition relation** $\delta \subseteq Q \times (\Sigma \cup \{\epsilon\}) \times \mathbb{K} \times Q$.

Three modifications have been made with respect to the earlier definition of FSAs in subsection 1.3.1 above. First, WFSAs are defined with respect to a particular semiring. Second, in place of the finite state set F there is a function ω which gives the **final weight** for each state. By convention, this is assumed to be a total function and a state $q \in Q$ is said to be non-final if $\omega(q) = \bar{0}$.[9] Third, the transition relation δ has been extended to include weights. A **path** through a weighted finite acceptor is a triple of

1. a state sequence $q_1, q_2, \ldots, q_n \in Q^n$,

2. a string $z_1, z_2, \ldots, z_n \in (\Sigma \cup \{\epsilon\})^n$, and

3. a weight sequence $k_1, k_2, \ldots, k_n \in \mathbb{K}^n$

subject to the constraint that $\forall i \in [1, n] : (q_i, z_i, k_i, q_{i+1}) \in \delta$. This constraint holds that there exists an arc from q_i to q_{i+1} that has the label z_i and weight k_i. A path is **complete** if

[9]Alternatively, one could define ω as a partial function in which $\omega[q] \downarrow$ if and only if state q is final.

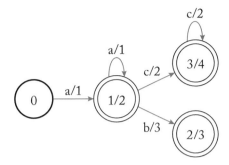

Figure 1.5: Weighted finite acceptor over the language $\{a\}^+(\{b\} \cup \{c\}^*)$.

1. $(s, z_1, k_1, q_1) \in \delta$ and

2. $\omega[q_n] \neq \bar{0}$.

That is, a complete path must also begin with an arc from the initial state s to q_1 with label z_1 and weight k_1 and halt in a final state, i.e., a state with a non-$\bar{0}$ final weight. Once again ignoring ϵ-labels, a WFSA accepts a string $z \in \Sigma^*$ with weight

$$\left(\bigotimes_{i=1}^{n} k_i \right) \otimes \omega[q_n] = k_1 \otimes k_2 \otimes \ldots \otimes k_n \otimes \omega[q_n],$$

if there exists a complete path with string z and weight sequence $k_1, k_2, \ldots, k_n$. Note that the **path weight**, the weight associated with a path, is given by the $\otimes$-product of the weight sequence and the final weight of the final state in the path.

An example WFSA is shown in Figure 1.5; weights are separated from arc and/or state labels by a forward slash. This WFSA accepts the string aacc, for example, with weight $1 \otimes 1 \otimes 2 \otimes 2 \otimes 4$, equal to 10 in the log and tropical semirings.

1.5.3   WEIGHTED REGULAR LANGUAGES

There are two roughly equivalent ways to define the **weighted regular languages** expressed by weighted finite acceptors. Under one definition, a weighted language is a partial relation over $\Sigma^* \times \mathbb{K}$; that is, it assigns weights to those strings in its language. However, one can alternatively define weighted languages as a total relation with $\bar{0}$ used as the weight for strings not accepted under the previous definition. This eliminates the distinction between those strings not accepted by the language and those accepted with weight $\bar{0}$.

1.6   WEIGHTED TRANSDUCERS AND RELATIONS

Finite transducers and relations can also be extended to support weights.

1.6.1   WEIGHTED FINITE TRANSDUCERS

The definition of a **weighted finite-state transducer** (WFST) should be obvious from the preceding discussion, but is provided for completeness. A WFST is a seven-tuple consisting of

1. a finite set of states Q,

2. a start state $s \in Q$,

3. a semiring $(\mathbb{K}, \oplus, \otimes, \bar{0}, \bar{1})$,

4. a final weight function $\omega \subseteq Q \times \mathbb{K}$,

5. an input alphabet Σ,

6. an output alphabet Φ, and

7. a transition relation $\delta \subseteq Q \times (\Sigma \cup \{\epsilon\}) \times (\Phi \cup \{\epsilon\}) \times \mathbb{K} \times Q$.

Paths through a WFST are then four-tuples consisting of

1. a state sequence $q_1, q_2, \ldots q_n \in Q^n$,

2. a input string $x_1, x_2, \ldots, x_n \in (\Sigma \cup \{\epsilon\})^n$,

3. a output string $y_1, y_2, \ldots, y_n \in (\Phi \cup \{\epsilon\})^n$, and

4. a weight sequence $k_1, k_1, \ldots, k_n \in \mathbb{K}^n$

subject to the constraint that $\forall i \in [1, n] : (q_1, x_i, y_i, k_i, q_{i+1}) \in \delta$. A **complete path** is a path where

1. $(s, x_1, y_1, k_1, q_1) \in \delta$ and

2. $\omega[q_n] \neq \bar{0}$.

That is, a complete path must also begin with a transition from the initial state s to q_1 with input label x_1, output label y_1, and weight k_1, and halt in a final state. Once again, ignoring the presence of ϵ-labels in the input and output strings, a WFST **transduces** or **maps** from $x \in \Sigma^*$ to $y \in \Phi^*$ with weight $k \in \mathbb{K}$ so long as a complete path with path weight k, input string x, and output string y exists.

1.6.2   WEIGHTED RATIONAL RELATIONS

Each WFST corresponds to a **weighted rational relation**, a three-way partial relation over $\Sigma^* \times \Phi^* \times \mathbb{K}$, but in practice, such relations are often reinterpreted as two-way partial relations over $\Sigma^* \to \Phi^* \times \mathbb{K}$; that is, for a given input string, they yield pairs of an output string and an associated path weight. Weighted relations can alternatively be defined as total relations similarly to the alternative definition of weighted languages given in subsection 1.5.3.

FURTHER READING

Partee et al. (1993: ch. 1–3) give a gentle introduction to sets, pairs, relations, functions, and strings.

Hopcroft et al. (2008: ch. 2) formalizes finite acceptors, though they eschew both transducers and weights.

Comparable formalizations of WFSTs are given by Roark and Sproat (2007: ch. 1) and Mohri (2009).

Hopcroft et al. (2008: ch. 3) formalize connections between finite acceptors, regular languages, and regular expressions. Jurafsky and Martin (2009: ch. 2) and Eisenstein (2019: ch. 9) briefly discuss these connections.

Hopcroft et al. (2008: ch. 5–7) and Allauzen and Riley (2012) present an extension of finite automata known as **pushdown automata**, corresponding to the family of formal languages known as **context-free grammars** (Chomsky 1963).

CHAPTER 2

The Pynini Library

This chapter illustrates finite-state text processing using Pynini (Gorman 2016), an open-source Python library for finite-state text processing. Pynini is one of the two major libraries used for finite-state grammar development at Google. It marries efficient implementations of a wide variety of WFST algorithms with the convenience of the Python programming language. Pynini has seen wide adoption since its release; for example, it has been used to build text normalization grammars (Gorman and Sproat 2016, Ritchie et al. 2019) and grapheme-to-phoneme conversion models (Gorman et al. 2020, Lee et al. 2020) for dozens of languages.

The next section describes the basic design architecture of Pynini and related libraries. Readers less interested in these details are welcome to skip to section 2.2, which describes conventions used by Pynini. A basic familiarity with the Python language is assumed; readers who lack this familiarity should first consult one of the many textbooks on the subject.

2.1 DESIGN

Pynini, like several other finite-state toolkits, builds upon OpenFst (Allauzen et al. 2007), an open-source C++ library also developed at Google. The OpenFst library is an efficient, fast, and comprehensive general-purpose framework for WFST applications, and it has been used at Google and elsewhere to develop **automatic speech recognizers**, **text-to-speech synthesizers**, and **input method engines** (i.e., text entry systems for mobile devices), including those bundled with Android devices. At the lowest level, OpenFst provides classes—representing WFSTs—and functions—representing algorithms over WFSTs—templated on the semiring of the input FST(s). For instance, the following snippet contains a C++ template function which compiles an FSA from a string, placing each byte (i.e., char) on its own arc.

```
template <class Arc>
void CompileString(const std::string &s,
                   fst::VectorFst<Arc> *fst) {
  fst->DeleteStates();
  fst->AddStates(s.size() + 1);
  typename Arc::StateId state = 0;
  fst->SetStart(state);
  for (const char c : s) {
    fst->AddArc(state, Arc(c, c, state + 1));
    ++state;
```

```
  }
  fst->SetFinal(state);
}
```

In addition to templated functions and classes, OpenFst provides a second layer known as the scripting API. This layer does away with the template arguments using virtual dispatch for methods and a registration mechanism for functions. This allows the user to abstract away from the choice of semiring—at least for a set of pre-registered semirings—but is otherwise just as verbose as the lower layer. A Python extension module, pywrapfst, included with OpenFst, wraps the scripting API. This additional layer eliminates the need for compilation since Python is interpreted. Ignoring differences in syntax and naming conventions, a similar string compilation function, shown below, closely resembles the C++ version given above.[1]

```
def compile_string(s: bytes) -> pywrapfst.VectorFst:
    fst = pywrapfst.VectorFst()
    fst.add_states(len(s) + 1)
    state = 0
    fst.set_start(state)
    for c in s:
        fst.add_arc(state, pywrapfst.Arc(c, c, None, state + 1))
        state += 1
    fst.set_final(state)
    return fst
```

Pynini, a Python extension module, greatly simplifies many of the drudgeries of finite-state development. It includes several algorithms not included in OpenFst, including methods for converting between automata and strings (section 2.3), **range concatenation** (section 3.3) and **cross-product** (section 3.7) operators, general-purpose optimization routines (section 4.1), and **context-dependent rewrite rule compilation** (section 5.2), all key tools for finite-state grammar development. The built-in operations provided by Pynini largely eliminate the above snippets' low-level manipulation of a WFSTs' states and arcs in favor of high-level operators like composition, union, and so on.

2.2   CONVENTIONS

FSAs and FSTs can be thought of as subsets of WFSAs and WFSTs, respectively, whose weights are limited to $\{\bar{0}, \bar{1}\}$. By the same token, FSAs can be thought of as subsets of FSTs for which all transitions have the same input and output labels. Therefore, Pynini follows the practices of OpenFst in using a single Fst type, a weighted transducer, for all four types of finite automata

---

[1] Throughout, Python functions are annotated with the optional type hints introduced in Python 3.5. Those unfamiliar or uncomfortable with these annotations are welcome to ignore them.

discussed in chapter 1. Thus, a weighted FSA is merely a WFST for which all input and output labels happen to match, and similarly, an unweighted transducer is one which only uses the "free" weight $\bar{1}$ and/or the "infinite" weight $\bar{0}$.

2.2.1 COPYING

The Fst class uses **copy-on-write** semantics, meaning that the copy method is constant time and only produce deep copies if one of the copies is later mutated. The same is true for SymbolTable objects discussed below.

2.2.2 LABELS

Arc input and output labels are represented by non-negative integers, with ϵ represented by label 0. One may use symbol tables to map between integer labels and strings for display, debugging, and string conversion (see section 2.3) but symbol tables are otherwise ignored. Negative-valued labels, while permitted, are reserved for implementation and should generally be avoided.

2.2.3 STATES

States are represented by dense sequences of integers—**state IDs**—ranging from 0 to $|Q| - 1$. As formalized in subsection 1.3.1, at most one state may be designated as the start state. An empty FST—one with no states—uses the constant pynini.NO_STATE_ID (equal to -1) as its start state. Thus, the following snippet asserts that an FST f is non-empty.

```
assert f.start() != pynini.NO_STATE_ID
```

Each state is associated with a final weight; non-final states have an infinite final weight $\bar{0}$ and final states have a non-$\bar{0}$ weight. Thus, the following snippet asserts that state q in an FST f is non-final.

```
assert f.final(q) == pynini.Weight.zero(f.weight_type())
```

2.2.4 ITERATION

Pynini does not provide random access to states and arcs; they must be accessed using specialized iterators. These iterators are invalidated—i.e., are no longer safe to use—in the following scenarios.

1. An ArcIterator is invalidated if any arcs leaving that state are mutated.

2. A MutableArcIterator is invalidated if arcs leaving any other state are mutated.

3. A StateIterator is invalidated if the number of states is changed.

2.2.5   WEIGHTS

`Fst` instances are associated with a given semiring and arc type. Pynini includes three built-in arc types.[2] The `standard` arc type, the default, gives the tropical semiring, with weights stored as 32-bit IEEE 754 floating-point numbers; it is commonly used to simulate the Boolean semiring. The `log` arc type gives the log semiring, once again using 32-bit floats. Finally, the `log64` arc type also uses the log semiring but uses "double-precision" 64-bit floating-point numbers. Pynini's `arcmap` function can be used to convert between semirings. For instance, the following snippet makes a deep copy of an FST `f` and converts it to the log semiring.

```
g = pynini.arcmap(f, map_type="to_log")
```

Finally, one can retrieve an `Fst`'s semiring using the `arc_type` and `weight_type` instance methods. For example, the following snippet asserts that `f` has the `standard` arc type and weights over the associated `tropical` semiring.

```
assert f.arc_type() == "standard"
assert f.weight_type() == "tropical"
```

2.2.6   PROPERTIES

Each `Fst` instance bears a set of **properties**, assertions about the FST's topology, weights, and so on. Some properties are binary—either true or false—whereas others are ternary—they also have an "unknown" value. Unknown property values are set when some operation invalidates the value of a property, but recomputing the true value of this property would be computationally expensive. Properties are stored in a single 64-bit unsigned integer, making them somewhat challenging to directly access. Each named property is represented by a module-level constant, a **property mask**. Some property masks are the bitwise union of multiple sets of related properties, and users can construct their own compound property masks using the bitwise OR operator `|`. There are two ways to test whether some FST has a given set of properties, but in both cases one passes the property mask to the instance method `properties`, and then compare the property mask to the properties this method returns. The second argument to the `properties` method is a Boolean which specifies whether or not "unknown" properties are to be recomputed; depending on the property mask and the size of the FST, this recomputation may or may not be an expensive operation. When this argument is `True`, this tests whether the FST in question actually has the given property or properties; when it is `False`, it simply tests whether it is known to have the given property or properties. Some examples are given below.

- Asserts that `f` is cyclic:

    ```
    assert f.properties(pynini.CYCLIC, True) == pynini.CYCLIC
    ```

---

[2]One can recompile Pynini with support for additional semirings but this requires considerable C++ knowledge.

- Asserts that f is known to be cyclic:

```
assert f.properties(pynini.CYCLIC, False) == pynini.CYCLIC
```

- Asserts that f is an unweighted acceptor:

```
ua_props = pynini.ACCEPTOR | pynini.UNWEIGHTED
assert f.properties(ua_props, True) == ua_props
```

One can set FST properties using the set_properties method. The verify method tests whether an FST's properties are correct, as shown in the following snippet:

```
assert f.verify()
```

2.3   STRING CONVERSION

Finite-state automata represent sets of strings, and relations between strings. Naturally, then, finite-state grammar development requires one to convert strings into automata, or to extract strings from automata.

2.3.1   TEXT ENCODING

Imagine that one wishes to construct an automaton representing a single string. In a **string** or **chain automaton**,

1. the start state s is labeled 0,

2. the highest-numbered state is final and has no outgoing arcs, and

3. every other state q is non-final and has one outgoing arc to state $q + 1$.

String FSTs, by construction, have exactly one path and one (output) string. It is relatively straightforward to construct such an FST given a list of arc labels (and optionally, a final weight), but how does one convert a string to a list of arc labels, or inversely, a list of arc labels to a string?

Modern digital computers represent characters using low-precision integers, and strings as contiguous sequences of these integers. **Character encodings** define a bidirectional mappings between these numeric sequences and human-readable strings. Conversion from strings to number sequences is referred to as **encoding**, and from number sequences to strings as **decoding**. Character encodings predate digital computing by at least a century, having been used since the earliest days of telegraphy, and have even earlier roots in the cryptographic methods of antiquity. One of the most widely known character encodings is **ASCII** (the American Standard Code for Information Interchange), first published in 1963. ASCII defines a set of 128 distinct "characters". These include

- 26 uppercase Latin letters,

- 26 lowercase Latin letters,

- 10 Arabic numerals,

- 33 punctuation characters,

- and 33 **control characters**.

The control characters are used for a variety of functions such as delimiting the start of a new line, but some are obsolete telegraphy signals. The full ASCII table is shown in Table 2.1. While ASCII is sufficient for most English text, it does not support diaeresis (e.g., *Brontë, coöperate, Häagen-Dazs, Motörhead, naïve*) or other commonly used Latin-script diacritics.

ASCII is a 7-bit encoding scheme because it defines 128 ($= 2^7$) unique symbols. However, ASCII characters are usually stored in bytes, which have 256 ($= 2^8$) distinct values. This extra bit is exploited by **ISO/IEC 8859**, an encoding standard published incrementally from 1987–2001. Each of the 16 encodings in this standard adds up to 128 additional characters to ASCII. For example, the Part 1 encoding, sometimes called "Latin-1", covers most of the Latin scripts of Western Europe, although it lacks a handful of characters used in Catalan, Danish, Dutch, Estonian, Finnish, French, German, Hungarian, and Welsh; a later revision, Part 15, fills some of these gaps and adds the Euro sign €. Part 2 covers central European languages that use the Latin alphabet. Other ISO/IEC 8859 encodings cover Hebrew, Greek, and various European languages written in Cyrillic. However, the ISO/IEC 8859 encodings have several major limitations. First, they only cover a tiny number of the alphabetic scripts in existence, and with the exception of Thai, make no effort to cover the indigenous scripts of Asia. Second, they provide no mechanism for specifying which of the 16 encodings was used for a given document. It is often possible to guess or "sniff" a document's encoding (e.g., Li and Momoi 2001), though such methods are necessarily heuristic. Finally, they provide no mechanism for mixing or switching between scripts. Each ISO/IEC 8859 encoding is a superset of ASCII, so one can mix English and Cyrillic using the Part 5 encoding, for example, but there is no way to combine Cyrillic and French, or Greek and Hebrew, for example.

The Unicode Consortium, a non-profit organization incorporated in 1991, was founded to address the deficiencies of earlier encoding standards. The consortium, working in concert with tech companies and international standards organizations, has produced over a dozen versions of their standard, **Unicode**. Unicode defines a universal character set of over one million distinct codepoints. Roughly 140,000 of these codepoints are currently in use, covering 154 modern and historical scripts at the time of writing. It also contains a huge number of non-linguistic symbols including those used in linguistics, mathematics, and music, various geometric shapes and arrows, and **emoji**. Because Unicode is designed for backward compatibility with many earlier standards, there may be more than one Unicode representation for a given string. For example, diacriticized Latin characters like *é*, can either be a character in its own right or an *e* plus a combining acute diacritic. Similarly, in the Latin script used to write Serbo-Croatian,

Table 2.1: The ASCII encoding; control characters are indicated by angle brackets.

0	<NUL>	32		64	@	96	`
1	<SOH>	33	!	65	A	97	a
2	<STX>	34	"	66	B	98	b
3	<ETX>	35	#	67	C	99	c
4	<EQT>	36	$	68	D	100	d
5	<ENQ>	37	%	69	E	101	e
6	<ACK>	38	&	70	F	102	f
7	<BEL>	39	'	71	G	103	g
8	<BS>	40	(	72	H	104	h
9	<TAB>	41	)	73	I	105	i
10	<LF>	42	*	74	J	106	j
11	<VT>	43	+	75	K	107	k
12	<FF>	44	,	76	L	108	l
13	<CR>	45	-	77	M	109	m
14	<SO>	46	.	78	N	110	n
15	<SI>	47	/	79	O	111	o
16	<DLE>	48	0	80	P	112	p
17	<DC1>	49	1	81	Q	113	q
18	<DC2>	50	2	82	R	114	r
19	<DC3>	51	3	83	S	115	s
20	<DC4>	52	4	84	T	116	t
21	<NAK>	53	5	85	U	117	u
22	<SYN>	54	6	86	V	118	v
23	<ETB>	55	7	87	W	119	w
24	<CAN>	56	8	88	X	120	x
25	<EM>	57	9	89	Y	121	y
26	<SUB>	58	:	90	Z	122	z
27	<ESC>	59	;	91	[	123	{
28	<FS>	60	<	92	\	124		
29	<GS>	61	=	93	]	125	}
30	<RS>	62	>	94	^	126	~
31	<US>	63	?	95	_	127	<DEL>

digraphs such as *dž*, *lj*, and *nj* are sometimes considered single characters, and in Korean, each hangul glyph represents a full syllable but can also be represented by their constituent jamo, each roughly a phoneme. In all three cases, Unicode supports both "composed" and "decomposed" representations of the above characters. For instance, *é* can be represented as a single codepoint (U+00E9) or as *e* (U+0065) followed by a combining acute accent (U+00E9). In Python, one can convert between various **Unicode normalization forms** using the normalize function from the built-in unicodedata module.[3]

Unicode defines several encodings for its character set. One, **UTF-32**, uses four bytes to represent all Unicode characters. However, this is massively inefficient, particularly for texts that consist primarily of Latin characters, and motivates an alternative encoding known as **UTF-8**. In this encoding, each character is encoded by one to four bytes, depending on the script. UTF-8 is backward-compatible with ASCII, in the sense that ASCII characters have the same encoding in both systems. Most non-ASCII Latin characters and characters from alphabets—Armenian, Greek, Cyrillic, etc.—require two bytes. Most of the remaining characters are encoded with three bytes; only rare East Asian characters, mathematical symbols, and historical scripts require four bytes to encode. At time of writing, UTF-8 is the most commonly used encoding, accounting for upward of 95% of all web pages at time of writing, and is the default encoding for most modern computers.

2.3.2   STRING COMPILATION

In Python 3, the str type represents a sequence of Unicode codepoints.[4] Pynini's accep function is used to compile a single Python str into a string Fst, an acyclic acceptor (in the sense of subsection 1.3.1) with a single final state and a single arc leaving each non-final state. It takes an input string argument and parses it according to the specified token_type, i.e., string parsing mode. Pynini provides three such modes. In all three modes, one can optionally specify the arc type (using the arc_type argument; this defaults to "standard", i.e., the tropical semiring) or the final weight for the string (using the weight argument; this defaults to $\bar{1}$ in the appropriate semiring).

In byte mode, the default mode, the string is encoded as a UTF-8 string and each arc contains a single byte. In utf8 mode, however, each arc contains a single Unicode codepoint (here specified in decimal).[5] The two modes are illustrated in Figure 2.1, which shows FSAs encoding a Unicode string in both byte and utf8 mode. Note that since UTF-8 is a superset of ASCII, there is no distinction between byte and utf8 modes for strings composed solely of ASCII characters.

Both byte and utf8 modes use special conventions for interpreting the ASCII square bracket characters [and]. In the most common case, any string surrounded by [on its left

---

[3]https://docs.python.org/3/library/unicodedata.html#unicodedata.normalize
[4]This is a departure from Python 2, in which str is a bytestring.
[5]The somewhat unintuitive name for this mode comes from the use of UTF-8 as an intermediate encoding.

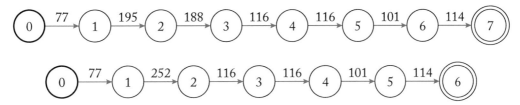

Figure 2.1: The German word *Mütter* 'mothers' compiled into a string in byte (above) and utf8 (below) modes. In byte mode, *ü* is encoded using two arcs (labeled 195 and 188, the decimal representation of its UTF-8 encoding), but in utf8 mode only one (252, the decimal representation of its Unicode codepoint) is needed.

and] on its right is taken to be an decimal or hexidecimal integer and is processed by the C standard library function stroll. If this routine succeeds, the integer is used as an arc label and the enclosing square brackets are subsequentially ignored. For example, in both byte and utf8 modes, strings abc, [97][98][99], and [0x61][0x62][0x63] all give rise to the label sequence [97, 98, 99]. To prevent [and] from being interpreted as a delimiter for bracketed spans, rather than a literal character, one can "escape" them by adding a preceding backslash, and escaping can be automated using Pynini's escape function. The complete bracket parsing procedure is described in Appendix B.

The third mode, symbol table mode, is triggered by providing a SymbolTable, a bidirectional hash table mapping between strings and integers, as the token_type argument. In this mode, the string is assumed to consist of substrings separated by a space character, and each substring is assumed to be assigned to an integer label by the provided symbol table. Sample snippets are given below.

- Compiles string s in byte mode:

  ```
  f = pynini.accep(s)
  ```

- Compiles string s in UTF-8 mode with final weight 2:

  ```
  f = pynini.accep(s, token_type="utf8", weight=2)
  ```

- Compiles string s in symbol table mode using symbol table sym:

  ```
  f = pynini.accep(s, token_type=sym)
  ```

Whenever possible, Pynini functions and methods that expect FST arguments will implicitly cast str instances to Fst by calling the accep function on the input string. This allows one to, for example, construct an FSA representing the union of a set of strings by passing string arguments to the union function (section 3.4) without explicitly compiling those strings first.

Implicit casting from strings to FSAs is used throughout this book, and the `FstLike` type hint is used to label interfaces that support implicit string-to-FSA coercion.

Pynini provides two other methods for string compilation. Both create **string maps**, transducers constructed from the union of many input/output string pairs. The `string_file` function builds a string map FST from a **TSV** (tab-separated values) file. Rows of this file are interpreted as follows.

1. If a row contains one column, it is interpreted as both input and output string.

2. If a row contains two columns, the first is interpreted as the input and the second as the output string.

3. If a row contains three columns, the first and second are interpreted as input and output strings and the third as a final weight.

The `string_map` function works similarly but the strings and/or string tuples are passed as iterable Python objects rather than read from a text file. Both functions use a **prefix tree** construction which gives a much more compact FST than would be obtained using the naïve approach. For both functions, one may optionally specify an `arc_type`, or select non-default string compilation modes for the input and/or output using the `input_token_type` and `output_token_type` arguments. The following snippet illustrates compilation of a string map FST mapping between U.S. state abbreviations and state names.

```
f = pynini.string_map(
    [
        ("AL", "Alabama"),
        ("AK", "Alaska"),
        ("AR", "Arkansas"),
        ("AZ", "Arizona"),
        ("CA", "California"),
        ...
        ("WY", "Wyoming"),
    ]
)
```

2.3.3   STRING PRINTING

Two mechanisms are available for extracting strings from automata. For string FSTs, a corresponding Python `str` can be extracted using the `string` method. Much like the `accep` function, `string` supports an optional `token_type` argument, and this has roughly the same semantics as before. An example snippet is shown below.

```
s = f.string(token_type="utf8")
```

However, the string method will raise an exception if the FST has multiple paths. In this case, one must instead iterate over the paths by calling the paths method, which returns an iterator over input and output strings. Much like the string_file and string_map functions, paths supports optional input_token_type and output_token_type arguments. At each step, the iterator computes the signature of a single path; it is advanced using the next method and rewound using the reset method; the done method returns True once all available paths have been traversed. At each step, one can use instance methods to extract

1. ilabels: the path's input string as a list of integer labels,

2. istring: the path's input string printed as per input_token_type,

3. olabels: the path's output string as a list of integer labels,

4. ostring: the path's output string printed as per output_token_type, or

5. weight: the weight of the path.

For example, the following snippet prints, for FST f, each output string and its corresponding path weight using symbol table sym.

```
paths = f.paths(output_token_type=sym)
while not paths.done():
    print(f"{paths.ostring()}:\t{paths.weight()}")
    paths.next()
```

The string paths iterator yields paths in a deterministic—but implementation-defined—order that is insensitive to path length and weight.

Path iteration cannot be applied to cyclic FSTs; by definition, such FSTs have an infinite number of paths, so iteration would never terminate. For cyclic transducers, one can create an acyclic approximation using the randgen function. For instance, the following snippet constructs an acyclic WFST containing 32 paths in f, randomly sampled by interpreting weights as negative log probabilities.

```
g = pynini.randgen(f, npath=32, select="log_prob")
```

Alternatively, one can extract the path(s) with the highest weight(s) using the shortestpath function (section 4.3). In either case, one can extract a list of output strings using the path iterator's ostrings method, which returns a generator over the output strings. For example, the following constructs a list of the output strings of an FST f.

```
ostrings = list(f.paths().ostrings())
```

In byte and utf8 mode, string printing ignores arcs with the 0 label used to indicate ϵ because this label corresponds to the ASCII control character \0, used to delimit the end of a string. However, ϵ-labels are printed in symbol table mode so long as the provided symbol table maps the label 0 to some non-empty string.

2.4   FILE INPUT AND OUTPUT

FSTs   `Fst` instances can be serialized (i.e., saved as files) in a binary, human-non-readable format using the `write` instance method, and deserialized (i.e., loaded from files) using the `Fst.read` class method, as in the following example snippets.

- Saves the FST `f` to the file `f.fst`:

  ```
  f.write("f.fst")
  ```

- Loads an FST from the file `f.fst` and assigns it to `f`:

  ```
  f = pynini.Fst.read("f.fst")
  ```

FARs   Some applications call for the use of an indexed collection of multiple FSTs stored in a FAR ("FST ARchive") file. FAR files consist a brief header followed by a sequence of serialized FSTs, each associated with a string key. In Pynini, one can read from or write to FAR files using the `Far` class, as shown in the following snippets.

- Creates a new FAR `f.far` and writes the FST `g` to it:

  ```
  with pynini.Far("f.far", "w") as writer:
      writer["g"] = g
  ```

- Opens an existing FAR `f.far` and reads the FST `g` from it:

  ```
  with pynini.Far("f.far", "r") as reader:
      g = reader["g"]
  ```

Symbol tables   `SymbolTable` instances also have a binary serialization but are more often stored in a human-readable TSV format with the symbol string in the first column and the associated integer arc label in the second. One can serialize a symbol table in this format with the `write_text` instance method and deserialize it with the `SymbolTable.read_text` class method, as shown below.

- Saves the symbol table `s` to the file `s.sym`:

  ```
  s.write_text("s.sym")
  ```

- Loads a symbol table from the file `s.sym` and assigns it to `s`:

  ```
  s = pynini.SymbolTable.read_text("s.sym")
  ```

2.5   ALTERNATIVE SOFTWARE

Finite-state grammar development software has been widely available since the early 1990s (Antworth 1990), and Pynini is just one of many finite-state toolkits in wide use. One closely related library is Thrax (Roark et al. 2012).[6] The Xerox finite-state toolkit (Beesley and Karttunen 2003) is the inspiration for several modern clones, including Foma (Hulden 2009), HFST (Lindén et al. 2009), and Kleene (Beesley 2012). What differentiates Pynini from these other tools is that it is fully embedded in Python and as such inherits that language's "multi-paradigmatic" flavor. Pynini FST operations can be combined with imperative, functional, and object-oriented programming styles as desired. In contrast, tools like Thrax use a declarative, domain-specific language for finite-state grammars and lack constructs like conditionals, loops, mutable variables, and arrays. Furthermore, tools like Thrax cannot be used at runtime to compile, combine, or search WFSTs. Pynini code can even be executed concurrently using Python's built-in `multiprocessing` module.[7]

FURTHER READING

For further information about the design of OpenFst and Pynini and comparison with other libraries, see Allauzen et al. 2007 and Gorman 2016, respectively.

Pynini installation instructions can be found in Appendix A. Moran and Cysouw (2018) provide an introduction to Unicode for linguists.

---

[6]This is named for the ancient Greek grammarian Dionysus Thrax, credited with the discovery of parts of speech.
[7]https://docs.python.org/3/library/multiprocessing.html

CHAPTER 3

Basic Algorithms

This chapter describes key operations over finite-state automata. These include three known as the **rational algorithms**—concatenation, closure, and union—and several others used to combine automata. More advanced algorithms are described in the following chapter. In both this and the following chapter, an algebraic characterization, an informal description of the topology of the resulting automaton, and example code snippets are provided for each algorithm.

Some automata algorithms, such as composition and determinization, described in the following chapters, are **constructive**, meaning that they produce a new automaton. Other algorithms, such as concatenation, closure, and union, are naturally expressed as **destructive** algorithms which work in place, mutating one of the input automata. For some algorithms, both constructive and destructive variants exist. In Pynini, constructive algorithms are expressed as module-level functions and return a new automaton. For instance, the following constructs an equivalent deterministic automaton d, as defined in the following chapter, from the non-deterministic automaton n without mutating n.

```
d = pynini.determinize(n)
```

In contrast, destructive algorithms are invoked using instance methods of the Fst class. For example, the following snippet concatenates (i.e., appends) automaton g to automaton f, mutating f.

```
f.concat(g)
```

However, note that in Pynini, destructive algorithms can also be invoked constructively using module-level functions. These functions simply make a copy of the input automaton, apply the destructive algorithm, and return the resulting automaton. For example, the following snippet computes the concatenation of automata f and g without mutating either argument.

```
fg = pynini.concat(f, g)
```

Wherever possible, destructive methods return a reference to the mutated automaton to permit chaining. For example, the following snippet computes the optimized closure of automaton f.

```
f.closure().optimize()
```

Finally, operations which return something other than automata may either be implemented as module-level functions or as instance methods of the Fst class.

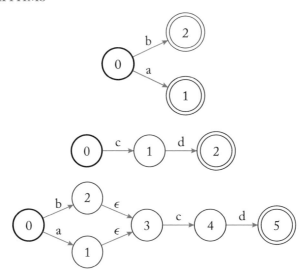

Figure 3.1: Finite acceptors for the regular languages {a, b} (above), {cd} (center), and their concatenation (below).

3.1 CONCATENATION

The regular languages are closed under concatenation, so the concatenation of any two regular languages is itself a regular language. It is straightforward to generalize the definition of concatenation in subsection 1.3.2 to the weighted rational relations and to intermediate subclasses such as the rational relations and weighted regular languages, all of which are also closed under concatenation. For instance, while a weighted relation μ transduces string a to string b with weight k_μ and ν transduces c to d with weight k_ν, their concatenation $\mu\nu$ transduces ac to bd with weight $k_\mu \otimes k_\nu$.

It is also straightforward to compute the concatenation of two or more WFSTs. Let $F_A \subseteq Q_A$ and ω_A be the set of final states, and the final weight function, respectively, for automaton A, and let s_B be the start state for automaton B. Then, to form their concatenation AB, one simply adds an ϵ-arc from every state $q \in F_A$ to s_B with weight $\omega_F[q]$, and sets $\omega_F[q] \uparrow$. In other words, one connects the final states of the left-hand side automaton to the start state of the right-hand side automaton. This is illustrated in Figure 3.1. Since this construction necessarily introduces ϵ-arcs, one may wish to perform ϵ-removal after concatenation.

In Pynini, concatenation is implemented by the concat method, which mutates its left-hand side argument. The addition operator + and the addition-assignment operator += are also overloaded to implement concatenation of Fst objects. Some example snippets are given below.

- Destructively appends b to a:

```
a.concat(b)
```

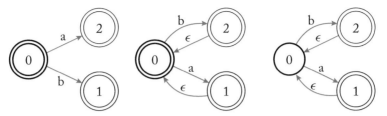

Figure 3.2: Finite acceptors for the regular languages $\{a, b\}^?$ (left), $\{a, b\}^*$ (middle), and $\{a, b\}^+$ (right).

- Concatenates a and b, overwriting a:

  ```
  a += b
  ```

- Concatenates a and b without mutation:

  ```
  ab = pynini.concat(a, b)
  ```

- Concatenates a, b, and c without mutation:

  ```
  abc = a + b + c
  ```

3.2   CLOSURE

The **closure** of a regular language, as defined in subsection 1.3.2, consists of all possible concatenations of the language with itself. Once again, there is a generalization of this definition to weighted rational relations and intermediate subclasses. For example, if a weighted relation μ transduces a to b with weight k, then μ^+ transduces from a to b with weight k, from aa to bb with weight $k \otimes k$, from aaa to bbb with weight $k \otimes k \otimes k$, and so on. μ^* is defined similarly to μ^+ but also transduces from ϵ to ϵ with weight $\bar{1}$.

It is simple to construct the closure of a finite automaton. Given automaton A with start state s, final states $F \subseteq Q$, and final weight function ω, A^+ is obtained by adding an ϵ-arc from every state $q \in F$ to s with weight $\omega[q]$, and A^* is built from A^+ by additionally setting $\omega[s] = \bar{1}$, i.e., by marking the start state final. This construction is illustrated in Figure 3.2.

In Pynini, closure is implemented by the destructive method closure. The Fst properties star, plus, and ques are provided as aliases for constructively computing X^*, X^+, and $X^?$, respectively. Some example snippets are given below.

- Destructively computes the $*$-closure of f:

  ```
  f.closure()
  ```

- Constructively computes the $*$-closure of f:

```
f_star = pynini.closure(f)
```

- Constructively computes the +-closure of f:

```
f_plus = f.plus
```

3.3   RANGE CONCATENATION

Range concatenation is a generalization of concatenation and closure. Recall the concatenation notation X^n where X is a language and $n \in \mathbb{N}$ where $\mathbb{N}$ is the set of counting numbers $\{1, 2, \ldots\}$, introduced in subsection 1.2.3. This notation is easily generalized to weighted relations and their subclasses. Now, let $X^{m,n} = \bigcup_{i=m}^{n} X^i = X^m \cup X^{m+1} \cup \ldots \cup X^n$ where $m \in \{0\} \cup \mathbb{N}$ and $n \in \mathbb{N} \cup \{\infty\}$, so that m and n act as (inclusive) ranges for the number of concatenations, noting that $X^{m,m} = X^m$ for $m \in \mathbb{N}$. Informally, one can construct the **range concatenation** of a transducer by first computing the closure if $n = \infty$, then repeatedly concatenating the transducer with itself, marking intermediate start states as final. As before, this procedure may introduce ϵ-arcs so one may wish to apply ϵ-removal afterward.

In Pynini, the power operator `**` is overloaded to compute n-concatenation and range concatenation. For n-concatenation the "exponent" is a single positive integer, and for range-concatenation, the exponent is a two-tuple (m, n) where m is a non-negative integer lower bound and n, the upper bound, is either a positive integer or ..., Python's built-in ellipsis literal, the latter indicating an infinite upper bound. Some example snippets are given below.

- Computes the 4-concatenation of f:

```
f4 = f ** 4
```

- Computes the $(5, 7)$-concatenation of f:

```
f5to7 = f ** (5, 7)
```

- Computes the $(3, \infty)$-concatenation of f:

```
f3plus = f ** (3, ...)
```

3.4   UNION

The regular languages are also closed under union, and it is straightforward to generalize the definition of union given in subsection 1.3.2 to weighted rational relations and intermediate subclasses. For example, if a weighted relation μ transduces string a to b with weight k_μ and ν transduces c to d with weight k_ν, then their union $\mu \cup \nu$ transduces a to b with weight k_μ and from c to d with weight k_ν.

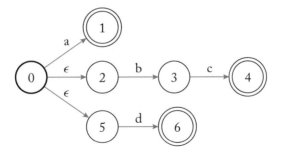

Figure 3.3: Finite acceptor for the regular language {a} ∪ {bc} ∪ {d}.

The union of two or more finite automata can be constructed, once again, by connecting the two with ϵ-arcs. Given automata A, B with start states s_A and s_B, their union is formed by adding an ϵ-arc from s_A to s_B or, equivalently, from s_B to s_A. An example is shown in Figure 3.3. This algorithm can be applied to arbitrarily many automata, and the ϵ-arcs it introduces can be eliminated with ϵ-removal (see subsection 1.3.1).

In Pynini, union is implemented by the method `union`, which mutates its left-hand side argument. The OR operator `|` and the OR-assignment operator `|=` are also overloaded to compute the union of `Fst` objects. Below are a few example snippets.

- Computes the union of a and b, destructive on a:

  ```
  a.union(b)
  ```

- Computes the union of a, bc, and d without mutation:

  ```
  a_bc_d = pynini.union(a, bc, d)
  ```

- Computes the union of a, bc, and d without mutation:

  ```
  a_bc_d = a | bc | d
  ```

The `string_file` and `string_map` methods, introduced in subsection 2.3.2, provide alternatives to union; they are more efficient when constructing the union of a large number of strings or string input/output pairs.

3.5   COMPOSITION

Intersection, defined in subsection 1.2.1, can be generalized to weighted regular languages. For example, if a weighted language M accepts a with weight k_M and N accepts a with weight k_N, then their intersection $M \cap N$ accepts a with weight $k_M \otimes k_N$. Intersection of weighted acceptors, the automaton characterization of the weighted regular languages, is also well-defined. In Pynini, it is computed constructively by the `intersect` function. However, rational relations are not closed under intersection. Intersection is one of several WFST algorithms implemented via composition, which is now described.

Composition is a generalization of intersection and relation chaining. Its precise interpretation depends on whether the inputs are languages or relations. As discussed above, the composition of two languages M and N yields the intersection $M \cap N$. The composition of a language M and a relation ν, written $M \circ \nu$, yields the relation $\{(a, b) \mid a \in M \land b \in \nu[a]\}$. That is, composition restricts the domain of the relation via intersection with the left-hand side language. Similarly, composition of a relation μ and language N, written $\mu \circ N$, yields the relation $\{(a, b) \mid b \in \mu[a] \land b \in N\}$, restricting the range of the relation via intersection with the right-hand side language. Finally, the composition of two relations μ, ν, written $\mu \circ \nu$, yields the relation $\{(a, c) \mid b \in \mu[a] \land c \in \nu[b]\}$; in other words, it yields a relation which chains the output of μ to the input to ν. The weighted rational relations and their subclasses are closed under composition, as are weighted finite transducers. Thus, the composition of two or more finite automata are themselves finite automata.

Composition is associative, and n-ary composition can be implemented by a sequence of two-way compositions. Note, however, that for automata, one bracketing into a sequence of two-way compositions—e.g., $A \circ B \circ C$ factored as the **left-associative** $(A \circ B) \circ C$ vs. the **right-associative** $A \circ (B \circ C)$—may be far more efficient than other equivalent associativities, and it is an open question how to optimally factor an n-ary composition into a sequence of $n - 1$ two-way compositions. In this text, left-associativity is assumed except where specified with parentheses.

Whereas previously discussed algorithms run in linear (or better) time proportional to the size—i.e., the number of states and arcs—of their inputs, composition may be far more expensive, depending on properties of the input automata.

Composition is illustrated in Figure 3.4, which shows the composition of two transducers, henceforth A and B, with start state s_A, s_B and associated transition relations δ_A, δ_B, respectively. During composition, one stores pairs of states—one from the left-hand side automaton and one from the right-hand side—in a queue, henceforth T; initially, the queue contains just the start state pair (s_A, s_B). One then repeatedly dequeues and processes pairs of states by matching the outgoing arcs of one of the two states with the other, using a procedure that resembles a game of Go Fish. That is, while processing a state pair, one state iterates over its outgoing arcs while the other state searches for an outgoing arc with the same "inside" label as the current arc. When the output labels of the left-hand state or the input labels of the right-hand state are already sorted, **bisection search**, a log-linear algorithm, can be used, and Pynini automatically applies arc-sorting before performing composition. More formally, suppose that one wishes to compute $A \circ B$ where δ_A, δ_B are the associated transition relations, and is currently processing the state pair (q_A, q_B), $(q_A, a, b, k_A, q_A') \in \delta_A$, that $(q_B, b, c, k_B, q_B') \in \delta_B$, so that an arc leaving q_A has an output label matching the input label of an arc leaving q_B. One then adds to the composed automaton an arc with input label a, output label c and weight $k_A \otimes k_B$ with a destination state

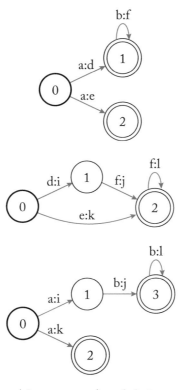

Figure 3.4: Two finite transducers (above, center) and their composition (below).

corresponding to the destination state pair (q'_A, q'_B). Finally, one enqueues the destination state pair in T so long it is neither being processed nor is already enqueued. This procedure halts when the queue is empty at the end of state processing. Note that additional logic is needed to process final states and ϵ-arcs. A trace of this procedure is given in Table 3.1.

Optimizing composition is something of a dark art, but generally speaking, one should sort arcs by their internal (i.e., output side of the left-hand automaton and input side of the right-hand automaton) labels, avoid internal ϵ-arcs, and prefer internal ϵ-arcs later along paths. Assiduous use of **composition filters** (Allauzen et al. 2010), the mechanism controlling interpretation of ϵ-arcs during composition, may produce substantial performance improvements, and may also reduce the size of the resulting automaton.

Pynini provides a compose function which computes the composition of two FSTs, and the matrix product operator @ is also overloaded to compute the composition of Fst objects. Both snippets below compute the composition of a and b.

- c = pynini.compose(a, b)

- c = a @ b

Table 3.1: Schematic trace of the composition depicted in Figure 3.4. Handling of final states and output state numbering have been omitted for simplicity.

	Pair	Queue	Action
1.		$(0, 0)$	dequeue
2.	$(0, 0)$		match d, emit a:i arc, enqueue $(1, 1)$
3.	$(0, 0)$	$(1, 1)$	match e, emit a:k arc, enqueue $(2, 2)$
4.	$(0, 0)$	$(1, 1), (2, 2)$	dequeue
5.	$(1, 1)$	$(2, 2)$	match f, emit b:j arc, enqueue $(1, 2)$
6.	$(1, 1)$	$(2, 2), (1, 2)$	dequeue
7.	$(2, 2)$	$(1, 2)$	dequeue
8.	$(1, 2)$		match f, emit b:l arc
9.	$(1, 2)$		halt

3.6 DIFFERENCE

The **difference** of two unweighted languages is well defined (subsection 1.2.1), though there is no comparable definition for relations nor for weighted languages, since semirings do not support negation or difference. Given languages M and N, $M - N$ denotes a set containing all strings of M which are not strings of N; that is, $M - N = \{a \mid a \in M \wedge a \notin N\}$. Note that unlike intersection and union (subsection 1.2.1), difference is not commutative. That is, $M \subseteq N$ implies that $M - N = \emptyset$ but it does not imply that $N - M = \emptyset$. The related notion of the **complement** of a language M denotes the difference $\Sigma^* - M$, that is the difference between the **universal language** and M.

In Pynini, difference is also implemented via composition and poses similar efficiency considerations. Pynini provides a difference function, and the subtraction operator is overloaded to compute the difference of Fst objects. Both snippets below constructively compute the difference of a and b.

- c = pynini.difference(a, b)

- c = a - b

3.7 CROSS-PRODUCT

The **cross-product** of two languages, defined in subsection 1.2.2, generalizes to weighted regular languages. If M accepts string m with weight k_M and N accepts n with weight k_N, their cross-product $M \times N$ transduces from m to n with weight $k_M \otimes k_N$.

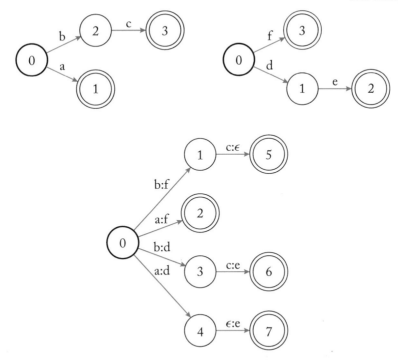

Figure 3.5: Finite automata for the regular languages {a, bc} (above left), {de, f} (above right), and their cross-product (below).

Cross-products of weighted acceptors can be efficiently computed via composition. If A and B are weighted acceptors, their cross-product is given by replacing their internal labels (i.e., the output labels of A and the input labels of B) with ϵ, removing any resulting ϵ-arcs, and then composing the resulting transducers using the appropriate composition filter. This produces the weighted relation $A \times B \times \mathbb{K}$. An example is shown in Figure 3.5. This algorithm is guaranteed to produce an optimal transducer (as defined below) in the common case in which A and B are both ϵ-free string acceptors.

In Pynini, one can compute the cross-product of two acceptors using the cross function, as shown in the following snippet.

```
c = pynini.cross(a, b)
```

3.8   PROJECTION

Projection is an operation defined over rational relations with or without weights. It converts a relation to a language over either the domain or range, something that is particularly useful when applying rewrite rules to strings (section 5.3). For example, if $\mu \subseteq \Sigma^* \times \Phi^* \times \mathbb{K}$ is a weighted

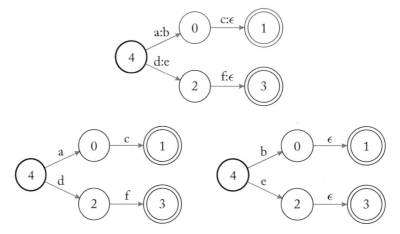

Figure 3.6: Finite automata for the rational relation ({ac} × {b}) ∪ ({df} × {e}) (above), and its input (below left) and output (below right) projections.

rational relation mapping from a to b with weight k, then its **input projection**, $\pi_i(\mu) \subseteq \Sigma^* \times \mathbb{K}$, is a weighted regular language that accepts a with weight k. Similarly, its **output projection**, $\pi_o(\mu) \subseteq \Phi^* \times \mathbb{K}$, is a weighted regular language that accepts b with weight k. These definitions also generalize to unweighted inputs.

It is straightforward to compute the projections of a transducer. The input projection is computed simply by replacing the output label of every arc with its input label, and the output projection is computed by replacing the input label of every arc with its output label. An example is shown in Figure 3.6.

In Pynini, the `Fst` object has a destructive `project` method; the direction of projection is specified by passing either `"input"` or `"output"` as an argument.

3.9   INVERSION

Inversion is an operation defined over weighted or unweighted rational relations which inverts the direction of the underlying relation. For instance, let $\mu \subseteq \Sigma^* \times \Phi^* \times \mathbb{K}$ be a weighted rational relation that maps from a to b with weight k, then its inverse $\mu^{-1} \subseteq \Phi^* \times \Sigma^* \times \mathbb{K}$ is a relation which maps from b to a with weight k.

As with projection, it is straightforward to compute the inverse of an automaton: one merely swaps the input and output labels for every arc in the automaton.

In Pynini, the `Fst` object has a destructive `invert` method.

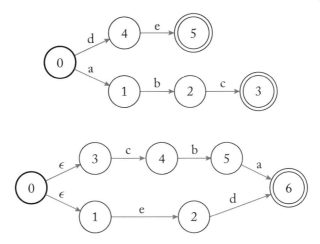

Figure 3.7: Finite automata for the regular language {abc, de} (above) and its reversal {cba, ed} (below); note that reversal introduces ϵ-arcs from a **superinitial** state.

3.10   REVERSAL

Regular languages and rational relations, both weighted and unweighted, are closed under **reversal**. This algorithm simply reverses the direction of the strings in a regular language, and the string pairs in a rational relation. For instance, the reversal of the relation {ab} × {cd} is {ba} × {dc}. More generally, if x^r is the reversal of the string x, then the reversal of a relation γ is defined as $\{(a^r, b^r) \mid (a, b) \in \gamma\}$.

Reversal of an automaton is linear in the number of states plus the number of arcs. In the weighted case, the weights on any string/pair of strings remain unchanged in the corresponding reversal. One complexity concerns the handling of automata which have multiple final states. Since the formalism used here requires that there be a single start state, one can imagine that the input to reversal has not multiple final states, but rather a single **superfinal** state reached by ϵ-transitions from the formerly final states. This superfinal state will be the start state in the reversed automaton. An example is shown in Figure 3.7.

Pynini provides a constructive `reverse` function.

FURTHER READING

The above algorithms for closure, concatenation, and union were proposed by Thompson (1968) in a report on the UNIX command-line utility `grep`.

Two algorithms that can be used to optimize composition are for optimization purposes are **epsilon-normalization** (`epsnormalize`), which produces an equivalent transducer such that all input (respectively, output) non-ϵ-labels precede all ϵ-labels along each path (Mohri 2002a), and **synchronization** (synchronize) which produces an equivalent transducer which "synchronizes" the position of input and output ϵ-labels along each path (Mohri 2003).

Allauzen et al. (2007) and Mohri (2009) provide brief summaries of other algorithms supported by Pynini.

CHAPTER 4

Advanced Algorithms

This chapter describes several other important operations over finite-state automata. These include algorithms used to optimize and search automata.

4.1 OPTIMIZATION

There are many senses in which a finite automaton can be said to be "optimal" or "optimized". One sense, alluded to above, is that an automaton can be optimized for composition—since transducers are often built to be composed with other automata—by eliminating internal ϵ-labels or by moving ϵ-labels later along paths. Alternatively, an automaton can be optimized for space in memory, by reducing the number of states (and possibly, arcs). Indeed, modern mobile devices may contain megabytes' worth of WFSTs for text entry, spelling correction, speech recognition and synthesis, and so on, all compressed to minimize their footprint in memory.

Pynini provides a general-purpose optimization routine, the `optimize` method, based on the traditional notion of **minimality**. An automaton is **minimal** if it expresses its language or relation, weighted or unweighted, using the minimal number of states; by definition, then, every automaton either is minimal or is equivalent to a minimal automaton. Efficient algorithms exist for the minimization of many types of finite automata, with or without weights (Mohri 2000, Revuz 1992). However, these impose stringent prerequisites on inputs. To begin, the optimization procedure applies ϵ-removal if the input WFST is not known to be ϵ-free. It then applies the minimization procedure. Traditional minimization algorithms also require that the automaton be **deterministic**. Algorithms for **determinization**, i.e., finding an equivalent deterministic automaton, are among the most complex and computationally expensive finite-state algorithms, but they are crucial for real-time WFST-based systems such as automatic speech recognizers (e.g., Mohri 1997).

In subsection 1.3.1, the transition relation δ for acceptors was defined as a partial relation over source states Q, labels ($\Sigma \cup \{\epsilon\}$), and destination states Q. Let us reformulate this as a two-way relation $\delta' \subseteq Q \times (\Sigma \cup \{\epsilon\}) \rightarrow Q$. Then, an acceptor is **deterministic** if δ' is a function (subsection 1.2.2); i.e., if there is at most one arc with a given label leaving a given state. If a deterministic acceptor is ϵ-free, it is also **unambiguous**, meaning that there is one path generating each string in its language.

All **weighted cycles-free acceptors**—acyclic acceptors, unweighted acceptors, and cyclic acceptors which do not have weights other than $\bar{0}$ and/or $\bar{1}$ during their cycles—are determinizable over a wide variety of semirings (Mohri 2009). However, cyclic weighted automata may not be determinizable, and it is difficult to even determine whether the determinization algorithm, applied to a given weighted automaton, will terminate (Allauzen and Mohri 2003). For weighted cyclic acceptors, `optimize` therefore applies determinization and minimization to the acceptor viewed as if it were unweighted, which ensures that determinization will terminate. This is a heuristic—it does not guarantee minimality—but in practice it tends to result in an significantly smaller ϵ-free acceptor.

Determinism is similarly defined for transducers. Let us reinterpret the four-way partial transition relation δ given in subsection 1.4.1 as a two-way relation $\delta' \subseteq Q \times (\Sigma \cup \{\epsilon\}) \to (\Phi \cup \{\epsilon\}) \times Q$. Then, a transducer is said to be **input-deterministic**, **sequential**, or **subsequential** if δ' is a function, i.e., if there is at most one arc with a given input label leaving a given state. Note that this definition is equally applicable to acceptors represented as transducers, so an input-deterministic transducer that happens to be an acceptor is also deterministic. If an input-deterministic transducer is ϵ-free it is also a function from input strings to output strings. As with acceptors, not all transducers are determinizable; for example they may be **non-functional**—corresponding to a string relation which is not a function—and/or may have weighted cycles. Therefore `optimize` applies determinization and minimization to a transducer viewed as if it were an acceptor, and in the case that the transducer has weighted cycles, as if it were also unweighted. Once again, this heuristic ensures that the determinization algorithm will terminate, and tends to result in a significantly smaller transducer.

An example of this algorithm is given in Figure 4.1. As a further demonstration, the above algorithm is applied to a sample of 700 speech recognition word lattices derived from Google Voice Search traffic. These lattices were previously used by Mohri and Riley (2015) to evaluate an algorithm for automaton disambiguation. Each path in the lattices represents a single hypothesis transcription according to a production-grade automatic speech recognizer. The exact size of each input lattice size is determined by a probability threshold, i.e., paths whose probabilities fall below a certain threshold were pruned ahead of time. The lattices are acyclic and ϵ-free, non-deterministic, and weighted, and as such, the above optimization routine is guaranteed to produce a deterministic, minimal, ϵ-free acceptor. Each point in Figure 4.2 represents the size (in number of states) of one of these word lattices before and after optimization. As can be seen, optimization substantially reduces the number of states, particularly for the larger lattices, and the "after" automaton is never larger than the "before" automaton.

4.2 SHORTEST DISTANCE

The shortest distance problem arises in the implementation of many weighted automata applications. In finite-state automatic speech recognition, for example, it is a key component of **expectation maximization** training (Dempster et al. 1977) used to estimate automata weights from data.

Between any two states $q, r \in Q$, there are zero or more partial paths, each characterized by a weight sequence $k_1, k_2, \ldots, k^n \in \mathbb{K}^n$. Recall that the weight of each partial path is given

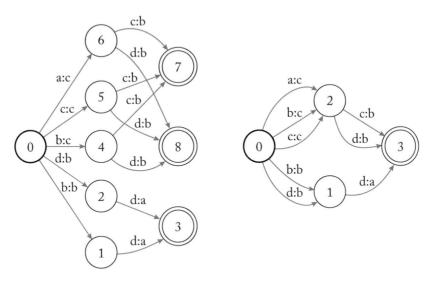

Figure 4.1: Finite transducer (left) and an equivalent transducer produced by applying the proposed optimization routine (right).

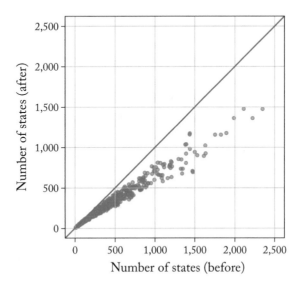

Figure 4.2: Number of states before (x-axis) and after (y-axis) optimization of speech recognizer word lattices using the proposed algorithm.

by the $\otimes$-product of the corresponding weight sequence $k = \bigotimes_{i=1}^{n} k_i$. The **shortest distance** between q and r is then given by the $\oplus$-sum of path weights P of all such partial paths $\bigoplus_{k \in P} k$. In practice, one is most often interested in paths that either begin in the initial state $s \in Q$ or end in a final state $f \in Q$ such that $\omega[f] \downarrow$. Let $\alpha \subseteq Q \times \mathbb{K}$ be the **forward distance**, a function from states to weights such that $\alpha[q]$ is the shortest distance from s to q not including the final weight $\omega[q]$. The **backward distance**, $\beta \subseteq Q \times \mathbb{K}$, is similarly defined: $\beta[q]$ is the shortest distance from q to the final states, but unlike α, also incorporates the final states' final weights. Thus, $\beta[s]$ is the shortest distance through the automaton. A state is said to be **accessible** if there exists a path to it from the initial state and **inaccessible** otherwise; similarly, a state is said to be **coaccessible** if there exists a path from it to a final state, and **coinaccessible** otherwise. Let us assume that α and β are both total functions and let $\alpha[q] = \bar{0}$ if q is inaccessible and $\beta[q] = \bar{0}$ if q is coinaccessible.[1]

In Pynini, the `shortestdistance` function returns a list of forward or backward distance weights. Some example snippets are given below.

- Compute the forward distance for `f`:

  ```
  alpha = pynini.shortestdistance(f)
  ```

- Compute the total shortest distance for `f`:

  ```
  total = pynini.shortestdistance(f, reverse=True)[f.start()]
  ```

4.3   SHORTEST PATH

The computation of the shortest path or paths is the key algorithm in the decoding of weighted automata such as those used for automatic speech recognition. There are two variants of the shortest path algorithm, both closely related to the notion of shortest distance. The **single shortest path** through an automaton is a subset of that automaton whose sole path has the same weight as the total shortest distance. Similarly, the **n shortest paths** through an automaton is a subset of that automaton containing just the n shortest paths. Both types of shortest path are only well-defined over semirings with the path property (subsection 1.5.1), such as the tropical semiring; without the path property, there is no guarantee that any path will have the same weight as the total shortest distance. An example of the shortest distance and shortest path algorithms is shown in Figure 4.3.

In Pynini, both shortest distance and shortest path procedures are guided by a **queue discipline**, automatically selected on the basis of the automaton's topology and semiring. For instance, the shortest path algorithm used with a **shortest-first** queue—used for cyclic automata over the tropical semiring—corresponds to Dijkstra's algorithm (Dijkstra 1959). In Pynini, the `shortestpath` function returns an acyclic automaton. Some example snippets are given below.

---

[1]Alternatively, one could define α and β as partial functions undefined for inaccessible and coinaccessible states, respectively.

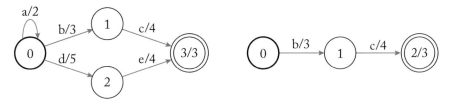

Figure 4.3: Finite weighted acceptor over the language {a}*({bc} ∪ {de}) (left) and its single shortest path {bc} (right). Assuming the tropical semiring, the shortest distances for the automaton on the left are $\alpha = 0, 3, 5, 7$ and $\beta = 10, 7, 7, 3$.

- Compute the single-shortest path for f:

  ```
  sp = pynini.shortestpath(f)
  ```

- Compute the eight shortest paths for f:

  ```
  sp = pynini.shortestpath(f, nshortest=8)
  ```

Note that tie resolution for the—single or nth—shortest path is deterministic but implementation-defined; for all intents and purposes it is unpredictable. A method for detecting ties in the shortest paths is described in subsection 5.3.2.

FURTHER READING

An early form of the optimization algorithm described above is proposed by Allauzen et al. (2004).

Mohri (2002b) describes the shortest distance and shortest path algorithms. Allauzen et al. (2007) and Mohri (2009) provide brief summaries of other algorithms supported by Pynini.

C H A P T E R   5

Rewrite Rules

The notion of a grammar as a relation between sets of strings is quite ancient. In the 4th century BCE, Pāṇini—Pynini's eponym—proposed a sophisticated computational system (see Penn and Kiparsky 2012) in which Sanskrit words and phrases are constructed by repeated application of **rewrite rules**. These rules consist of a target (for example, in Aṣṭdhyāyā 6.1.77, [i, iː, uː, ṛ, ṛː]), a replacement (the corresponding semivowels), and a context in which it is applied (before another vowel). Priscian, writing in the 6th century CE, proposes a system of rewrite rules generating inflectional variants of Latin verbs (Matthews 1972). In the 19th century, historical linguists—particularly those now known as the Neogrammarians—employed rewrite rules to describe language change. For instance, Grimm's Law correctly predicts that the initial *p in the Proto-Indo-European word meaning 'father' (cf. Latin *pater*) surfaces as [f] in Germanic (e.g., Old High German *fater*). In the 20th century, linguists adapted rewrite rules—some of which closely resemble historical sound changes—to sketch the morphophonemics of languages such as Menomini (Bloomfield 1939), Russian (Jakobson 1948), and Modern Hebrew (Chomsky 1951), and began to formalize rewrite systems. One particularly influential formal approach is the phonological rule notation popularized by Chomsky and Halle (1968). Subsequent work, reviewed below, establishes strong connections between the notation used by Chomsky and Halle and the rational relations,[1] provides algorithms to compile rewrite rules into finite-state transducers, and employs them for speech and language technology applications. This chapter formalizes rewrite rules and shows how they are compiled into finite transducers, combined into rule cascades, and applied to input strings. Their use is then illustrated with applications in speech and language technology, including **grapheme-to-phoneme conversion**, **morphological generation**, and **text normalization**; the latter two applications are discussed in greater detail in later chapters.

5.1   THE FORMALISM

This section defines **context-dependent rewrite rules**, a distillation of the formalism popularized by Chomsky and Halle's 1968 book *The Sound Pattern of English*, henceforth SPE. While the phrase "context-dependent" seems to suggest the family of formal languages known as the **context-sensitive languages**, this similarity is misleading. In fact, context-dependent rewrite rules as formalized below are equivalent to rational relations (Johnson 1972) and correspond

---

[1]In contrast, syntactic phenomena and the **transformational rules** used to describe them belong to higher classes of formal languages (see Shieber 1985 and citations therein).

to finite-state transducers. Furthermore, since FSTs are closed under composition, an ordered cascade of context-dependent rewrite rules can be composed into a single FST.

Before we proceed further, however, we need to clear up one possible misconception. Those familiar with SPE and phonological theories of slightly later vintage will also recall the notion of the morphophonological *cycle*, which played an important role in that theory of phonology. To wit, morphologically complex words were constructed affix-by-affix, and with each affixation process, a battery of phonological rules was applied to the (partially) constructed word. Under this model, a rule could in principle *apply to its own output*, a situation which in fact is not covered by Johnson's argument for equivalence. However this only becomes a problem if the number of cycles is unbounded. With a bounded number of cycles, one can always model the situation simply by composing the FST associated with a rule as many times as it needs to apply in the derivation. If, for the sake of simplicity, one has a single rule R, and assuming we represent the ith affixation process to the base B as $A_i(B)$, and assuming further that we have no more than k "cycles", then the resulting word can be computed as $B \leftarrow R \circ A_i(B)$, for $1 \leq i \leq k$.

If k is in principle *unbounded*, then there is a potential problem. This situation would obtain with a lexical FST that itself is *cyclic*—i.e., one where the graph that represents the FST has cycles, not to be confused with the linguistic notion of cyclicity just discussed. As far as we know, Hankamer (1989) was the first to emphasize the importance of such cases in finite-state morphology. Hankamer worked with data from Turkish, but in fact it is possible to construct theoretically unbounded cases even in English. Consider the productive derivational affixation process that makes verbs from adjectives by affixing *-ize*; the productive derivational process that turns verbs ending in *-ize* into nouns by affixing *-ation*; and the productive derivational process that makes adjectives from nouns by adding *-al*. These can be combined in a theoretically unbounded way:

- márginal

- márginalize

- marginalizátion

- marginalizátional

- marginalizátionalize

- marginalizationalizátion

- marginalizationalizátional

- marginalizationalizátionalize

- marginalizationalizationalizátion

- ...

Also marked, with an accent mark over the relevant vowel, is the location of the primary stress, which moves to the right as the complex word is built up. If one accepts the SPE theory that stress assignment is cyclic, then we would have a potentially unbounded morphological process where the stress assignment rule would apply to its own output at each affixation cycle. So while the morphology itself can in principle be handled by a finite state machine with cycles, the stress assignment rule could not be handled by a finite mechanism since the rule must be applied at each affixation point.[2] But as Hankamer (397) points out for Turkish, if one builds up long enough cycles of this kind "Turkish speakers and hearers tend to get confused", and the same is true for English constructions of the kind we discussed above. So unbounded cyclicity in the SPE sense is not really a practical problem.

But let us return to the main point. To begin let us consider a simplified version of the context-dependent rewrite rule formalism. Let Σ be the **alphabet**, the set of symbols over which the rule operates; note that whereas rational relations and finite transducers may have separate input and output alphabets, this is not permissible for rewrite rules. For phonological rules, Σ might consist of all phonemes (and, possibly, their allophones) in the given language; for a grapheme-to-phoneme rule, it would contain both graphemes and phonemes; and, for text generation or processing applications, might consist of all 256 bytes. If $s, t, l, r \in \Sigma^*$, then the following is a possible rewrite rule.

(1) $s \rightarrow t \; / \; l \underline{\quad} r$

In this formalism, $s \rightarrow t$ is the **structural change** and l and r is the **environment**. The final rule can be read as "s goes to t between l and r". By convention, one may omit an empty l and/or r, so that the following are also possible rules.

(2) $s \rightarrow t \; / \underline{\quad}$
       $s \rightarrow t \; / \; l \underline{\quad}$
       $s \rightarrow t \; / \underline{\quad} r$

Informally speaking, rule (1) specifies a rational relation with domain and range Σ^* such that all instances of *lsr* are replaced with *ltr* but all other substrings in Σ^* are passed through. For example, let $\Sigma = \{a, b, c\}$ and consider the following rule.[3]

(3) $b \rightarrow a \; / \; b \underline{\quad} b$

Some example input-output pairs for this rule are shown below.

---

[2]Needless to say, this is only a problem if one insists that stress assignment must be a cyclic process. In the case at hand, the problem can easily be addressed by, for example, assuming that each stressable affix, in this case *-ation*, comes with its stress marked. Then one would merely need a single rule applying on the fully formed word to destress, or demote the stress of preceding syllables.

[3]This example is adapted from Section 11.1 in Bale and Reiss 2018.

	bbba	$\rightarrow$	baba
(4)	abbbabbbc	$\rightarrow$	ababababc
	cbbca	$\rightarrow$	cbbca

In the last example, for instance, the conditions for application are not met so input and output are identical.

5.1.1 DIRECTIONALITY

However, the formalism developed so far does not specify how (3) is to apply to strings such as abbbba. This ambiguity arises from the fact that for this string, one application of the rule could block the application of the rule at another site. One might suppose that the rule is applied to all contexts that meet the structural description, regardless of whether the contexts overlap. In **simultaneous application**, both the third and fourth characters of the input string are flanked by b's, and both are transduced to a. Alternatively, one might instead suppose that the rule is applied by scanning the input string from the start to the end of the string, three segments at a time. In **left-to-right** or **right-linear application**, however, when the three-segment window is centered on the third segment—the second b— the structural description and environment are satisfied because at that point it is flanked by a b on both sides. Therefore, the rule is applied and that segment is mapped to a. However, the rule would not apply when this three-segment window was centered on the fourth segment because that b would no longer have a b to its immediate left. Finally, **right-to-left** or **left-linear application** applies the rule while scanning the input string from the end to the beginning. An example of applying (3) to an ambiguous string is shown below.

	simultaneous application:	abbbba	$\rightarrow$	abaaba
(5)	left-to-right application:	abbbba	$\rightarrow$	ababba
	right-to-left application:	abbbba	$\rightarrow$	abbaba

The three application directions correspond directly to where one will find the left-hand and right-hand environment for the rule, in the input or in the output. For a simultaneous rule, the left-hand and right-hand environments for an application must occur in the input. With a left-to-right rule, the left-hand environment must be in the output string and the right-hand environment must be in the input string; thus, a left-to-right rule application potentially affects an application of the same rule to a subsequent position in that it might create, or remove, a left-hand environment in the output for the next application of the rule. And a right-to-left rule is the reverse of a left-to-right rule: the left-hand environment must occur in the input and the right-hand environment in the output.[4]

---

[4]Thanks to Jeffrey Heinz for suggesting we present the differences in this way.

In SPE, all rules are assumed to apply simultaneously (op. cit., 343f.). However, Johnson (1972: ch. 5) adduces a number of phonological examples where directional application—either left-to-right or right-to-left, depending—is required. One example of this sort comes from Latin. In classical inscriptions, no distinction was made between [i, iː] and the front glide [j], or between [u, uː] and the back glide [w]; they are spelled *i* and *v*, respectively. Generally speaking, when an *i* or *v* occurs intervocalically—i.e., flanked by two other vowels—it is realized as a glide. Some examples are given below; note that *c* is [k], that intervocalic [j] is subsequently lengthened to [j.j], and that vowel length is not indicated orthographically.

	caveo	→	[ka.we.oː]	'I am careful'
(6)	ovis	→	[o.wis]	'sheep'
	peior	→	[pej.jor]	'worse'

What happens to a sequence of two or more intervocalic *i*'s and *v*'s? According to Steriade (1984), just the left-most eligible segment is read as a glide, as shown below.

	avia	→	[a.wi.a]	'grandmother'
(7)	lascivia	→	[las.kiː.wi.a]	'wantonness'
	pavio	→	[pa.wi.oː]	'I beat'

To obtain the correct result, the rules mapping intervocalic *i* and *v* to glides must be applied left-to-right. Were they applied simultaneously, for example, *avia* and *pavio* would erroneously surface as *[aw.ja] and *[paw.joː], respectively.

Note, however, that directionality of application has no discernable effect for perhaps the majority of rules, and can often be ignored.

5.1.2   BOUNDARY SYMBOLS

Let ^, \$ ∉ Σ be **boundary symbols** disjoint from Σ. Now let ^, the beginning-of-string symbol, to optionally appear as the left-most symbol in *l*, and permit \$, the end-of-string symbol, to optionally appear as the right-most symbol in *r*; the boundary symbols are not permitted to appear elsewhere in *l* or *r*, or anywhere within the structural description and change. Consider the following rule, a slight variant of (3).

(8)   b → a / ^ b __ b

To apply this rule, one must scan for string-initial instances of bbb and replace it with bab; given this specification, directionality is irrelevant. Example input-output pairs are given below.

	bbba	→	baba
(9)	abbbc	→	abbbc

Note that the rule does not apply in the latter case because the bbb sequence appears non-initially. Or, consider another variant of (3).

(10)   b → a / b __ $

To apply this rule, one must merely scan for string-final instances of bb and replace them with ba.

5.1.3   GENERALIZATION

Now consider a generalization of rewrite rules, in which a rewrite rule is specified by a five-tuple consisting of

1. an alphabet Σ,

2. a structural change $\tau \subseteq \Sigma^* \times \Sigma^*$,

3. a **left environment** $L \subseteq \{{}^\wedge\}^? \Sigma^*$,

4. a **right environment** $R \subseteq \Sigma^* \{\$\}^?$, and

5. a **directionality** (one of: "simultaneous", "left-to-right", or "right-to-left").

In other words, the structural change previously expressed by the strings s and t is now a rational relation, and the left and right environments previously expressed by strings l and r are now regular languages. The generalization about Latin intervocalic glides immediately above can be stated as a single rewrite rule (ignoring the lengthening of [j] to [j.j]) such that $\tau = \{(u, w), (i, j)\}$, L and R are the set of vowels $\{a, e, o, u, \ldots\}$, and direction of application is left-to-right.

5.1.4   ABBREVIATORY DEVICES

In the SPE tradition, the structural change and environment are usually specified as bundles of **phonological features**, an intensional specification of segments, rather than the extensional specifications of languages used above. For instance, [+Vowel] denotes the set of vowels, [+Vowel, +High] the set of high vowels, [+Vocalic, −Vowel] the set of glides, and so on. Using this notation, the intervocalic formation rule might be written roughly as follows:

(11) $\begin{bmatrix} +\text{Vocalic} \\ +\text{High} \end{bmatrix}$ → {−Vowel} / [+Vowel] __ [+Vowel]   (left-to-right)

Assuming a finite inventory of segments and a mapping from segments to their features, it is possible to compute the regular language extension for any featural specification. However, it is not always the case that a given regular language corresponds to a featural specification. For instance, consider the following feature system for the vowels of Turkish shown in Table 5.1. A

Table 5.1: Featural specification for the vowels of Turkish.

	[+Front]		[-Front]	
	[-Round]	[+Round]	[-Round]	[+Round]
[+High]	i	ü	ɪ	u
[-High]	e	ö	a	o

simple featural specification like [+Round] defines the set {ü, u, ö, o}; a complex featural specification bundle such as [+Front, +Round] gives the intersection [+Front] ∩ [+Round], the set of segments which are both front and round, namely {ü, ö}. All sets defined by the intersection of one or more featural specifications are known as **natural classes**. However, not all sets of the above vowels can be described in the above fashion: for instance, there is no featural specification corresponding to the set {e, o} under this feature system. Such classes are called **unnatural classes**.[5] However, in our opinion, the extensional notation's ability to express unnatural classes is no defect. When dealing with phonological processes, one can construct natural classes via intersection of extensionally defined sets of segments. Furthermore, linguists have encountered many cases in which a superficially similar series of phonological changes lack a unified expression under current mappings between features and phones. Finally, there is no obvious equivalent to featural specifications for an alphabet consisting of, for instance, orthographic characters rather than phonemic-phonetic symbols.

Linguists may be familiar with several other types of abbreviatory devices used in SPE and related work. One such convention are the **Boolean variables**, traditionally written with **Greek-letter variables**, ranging over {+, −} (Zwicky 1965). Johnson (1972: ch. 3) proves that under certain reasonable assumptions, this is a purely abbreviatory convention and does not increase the expressivity of the SPE formalism. Another such device is the **curly brace notation** used to express disjunctions of feature bundles and/or segments, and is equivalent to union. Finally, SPE uses **parentheses-schemata** to express certain long-distance processes such as stress assignment and related phenomena such as the reduction of weak syllables. The SPE schemata notation was widely critiqued at the time (e.g., Anderson 1974: ch. 9, Kenstowicz and Kisseberth 1977:189f., Piggott 1975) and subsequent technical developments, including directional rule application and the conception of prosodic-metrical structure as belonging to a separate representational tier (e.g., Hayes 1980, Idsardi 1992), have largely made this convention obsolete.

---

[5]Unnatural classes are by no means uncommon in phonological descriptions. For example, the Breton consonant mutation process known as **lenition** changes voiceless stops into the corresponding voiced stop (e.g., /t/ → /d/) and voiced stops into fricatives. However the set of fricatives produced does not form a natural class, since while /b/ changes to /v/, and /d/ changes to /z/, both voiced fricatives, /g/ changes to /x/, a voiceless fricative. Therefore, a simple rule that states that a [+Voice] stop becomes [+Continuant] will not do: one must add a special case for /g/.

5.1.5   CONSTRAINT-BASED FORMALISMS

We have little to say about **Optimality Theory** (OT; Prince and Smolensky 2004), **Harmonic Grammar** (Legendre et al. 2006), and related frameworks which formulate transductions using violable constraints and global optimization. It is generally believed that one can restrict the generation procedure ("Gen") and constraint set ("Con") so that all OT grammars correspond to an equivalent rational relation, and to an equivalent finite transducer (e.g., Eisner 1997, Heinz et al. 2009, Karttunen 1998), and it seems likely that similar equivalencies may hold between harmonic grammars, weighted rational relations, and weighted finite transducers. However, the proposed restrictions have largely been ignored by OT practitioners. Furthermore, we find that finite-state grammars based on rewrite rules—or a mixture of rules and constraints—tend to be more terse, and more easily understood and maintained, than those expressed via constraints alone.[6] Finally, it seems quite likely that standard forms of Optimality Theory are overly restrictive in their inability to express **opaque mappings** (in the sense of Chandlee et al. 2018) such as **counterfeeding** and **counterbleeding** (Kiparsky 1973).

5.2   RULE COMPILATION

Johnson (1972) proves that context-dependent rewrite rules are rational relations, and this result can be generalized to **weighted rewrite rules** by allowing τ, the structural change, to be a weighted rational relation (Mohri and Sproat 1996). Rules which apply only at the end or beginning of a string are generally trivial to express as a finite transducer. For example, consider the following rewrite rules, which prepend a prefix p or append a suffix s, respectively.

$$(12)\quad \begin{aligned} & \emptyset \rightarrow \{p\} \,/\, \{\char94\} \underline{\quad} \Sigma^* \\ & \emptyset \rightarrow \{s\} \,/\, \Sigma^* \underline{\quad} \{\$\} \end{aligned}$$

Such rules are equivalent to the rational relations $(\emptyset \times \{p\})\,\Sigma^*$ and $\Sigma^*\,(\emptyset \times \{s\})$, respectively. Greater difficulties arise from the possibility of multiple application with or without overlapping contexts for application, and the development of a general-purpose algorithm to compile (weighted) finite-state transducers from algebraic descriptions of rewrite rules proved quite challenging. Koskenniemi (1983), who developed one of the earliest finite-state grammars, a comprehensive description of Finnish morphophonology, used rewrite rules that were manually compiled into finite transducers, state-by-state and arc-by-arc. An early sketch of a rewrite rule compilation algorithm appeared in an unpublished 1981 lecture by Ronald Kaplan and Martin Kay, researchers at the Xerox Palo Alto Research Center (PARC), but was not published until much later (e.g., Kaplan and Kay 1994, Karttunen 1995).

---

[6]One example of this can be found in a study of stress in Shanghai compounds by Duanmu (1997); a rule-based analysis of the phenomenon fits on a single page whereas a roughly equivalent OT analysis of the same facts spans two dozen.

5.2.1   THE ALGORITHM

This section describes a generalization of the Kaplan and Kay-Karttunen rule compilation algorithm by Mohri and Sproat (1996). Their technique consists of the composition of five transducers, each a simple rational relation. For simplicity of explication we focus on left-to-right application, though minor variants of the algorithm produce right-to-left or simultaneous rules. First, if X is a language, let $\overline{X}$ denote its **complement**, the language consisting of all strings which are not elements of X; i.e., $\overline{X} = \{x \mid x \notin X\}$. Then, let $<_1, <_2, > \notin \Sigma$ be **marker symbols** disjoint from the alphabet Σ. Then, given a rule over Σ^* defined by structural change τ, left and right contexts L and R, the constituent transducers are defined as follows. (We remind the reader that π_i denotes the **projection** onto the input of a relation.)

1. ρ inserts the $>$ marker before all substrings matching R (i.e., it marks the beginnings of the righthand environment):
$$\emptyset \rightarrow > / \Sigma^*\_R.$$

2. ϕ inserts markers $<_1$ and $<_2$ before all substrings matching $\pi_i(\tau) >$:
$$\emptyset \rightarrow \{<_1, <_2\}/(\Sigma \cup \{>\})^*\_\pi_i(\tau)^7$$

3. γ applies the structural change τ anywhere $\pi_i(\tau)$ is preceded by $<_1$ and followed by $>$. It simultaneously deletes the $>$ marker everywhere. This transducer is schematicized in Figure 5.1.

4. λ_1 admits only those strings in which L is followed by the $<_1$ marker and deletes all $<_1$ markers satisfying this condition:
$$<_1 \rightarrow \emptyset / \Sigma^* L\_.$$

5. λ_2 admits only those strings in which all $<_2$ markers are not preceded by L and deletes all $<_2$ markers satisfying this condition:
$$<_2 \rightarrow \emptyset / \Sigma^* \overline{L}\_$$

In short, the ρ, ϕ, and γ transducers apply the τ transduction only between R and $<_1$; λ_1 guarantees that $<_1$ occurs only when preceded by L, and λ_2 guarantees that non-application occurs only when L does not precede. Then, the final context-dependent rewrite rule transducer is given by $\zeta = \rho \circ \phi \circ \gamma \circ \lambda_1 \circ \lambda_2$. An example is given in Figure 5.2.

To obtain right-to-left application, for example, one reverses the process: a λ transducer would insert a $<$ marker after all substrings matching L; ϕ would insert $>_1, >_2$ after all strings matching $< \pi_i(\tau)$; γ would apply the structural change to any τ preceded by $<$ and followed by $>_1$; ρ_1 would admit only those strings in which the $>_1$ marker is followed by R; and ρ_2 would admit only those strings in which $>_2$ is followed by $\overline{R}$, with ρ_1 and ρ_2 also deleting their respective markers. Then, $\zeta = \lambda \circ \phi \circ \gamma \circ \rho_1 \circ \rho_2$.

---

[7]This introduces two paths, one with $<_1$ and one with $<_2$, which ultimately correspond to the cases where L does and does not, respectively, occur to the left of the structural change (see steps 4–5).

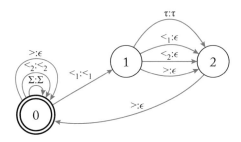

Figure 5.1: Schematic of the γ transducer, after Mohri and Sproat 1996, Figure 2. Note the arcs labeled with the regular language Σ and the rational relation τ; the corresponding automata must replace these arc to create γ.

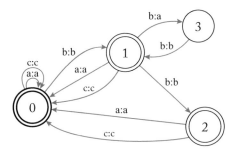

Figure 5.2: A transducer implementing the rewrite rule $\{b\} \times \{a\} / \{b\}$ ___ $\{b\}$ assuming left-to-right application and $\Sigma = \{a, b, c\}$.

One further detail is the handling of boundary symbols. When a boundary symbol is present in the context languages L or R, one can introduce them with a transducer $\beta = (\emptyset \times \{\wedge\}) \Sigma^* (\emptyset \times \{\$\})$, and remove them using the inverse transducer β^{-1}. Note that the boundary symbols are not members of Σ, but ζ must treat them much as any other symbol. Therefore, one must construct ζ using $\Sigma' = \Sigma \cup \{\wedge, \$\}$ in place of Σ. Then, the full construction is given by $\zeta' = \beta \circ \zeta \circ \beta^{-1}$.

Finally, Mohri and Sproat (1996) discuss the extension of the algorithm to the weighted case. In general τ can be a weighted transducer, meaning that a span of arcs introducing the output side of $\pi_o(\tau)$ will be weighted. If, for example, a final stop devoicing rule devoices a final stop 90% of the time, and leaves it voiced 10% of the time, one can model this with a τ that maps, say, /d/ to /t/ with probability semiring weight 0.9, and leaves it as /d/ with probability semiring weight 0.1. Then, in the appropriate string-final environment, an underlying /d/ will surface as /t/ with weight 0.9 and as /d/ with weight 0.1. For a cascade of weighted rules, implemented using composition, the weights of the individual rules are combined using semiring $\otimes$.

5.2.2 EFFICIENCY CONSIDERATIONS

The operations constructing the component transducers are relatively efficient, with one exception: rules introducing markers require the underlying acceptors to be deterministic. Consider a transducer which inserts a marker # after the regular language L; this corresponds loosely to several of the constituent transducers used by the Mohri and Sproat construction. In order to do this we need to construct a finite transducer that allows any sequence of characters in Σ^*, possibly including previous instances of L, and inserts # after L. Such a transducer is obtained by inserting an arc with an ϵ input label and a # output label after the final state(s) of L and marking the new destination state final. This requires that the input acceptor be deterministic so that for any string $l \in L$, there is but one path through the automaton; otherwise the string could bypass insertion of #. As mentioned above, determinization can be quite expensive, particularly if Σ is large or if L is complex. So, for example, if one would like to write a rule that inserts a given word after a set of words, and this latter set of words numbers in the tens of thousands, then the compilation of said rule will be somewhat slow and the resulting FST quite large. Fortunately there is usually a way around such problems. In the hypothetical example above, one could arrange for all words in one's list of interest to be pre-tagged already with some marker, and condition the rule's environment on that marker alone. This will result in more efficient compilation and application, and produce a more compact rule transducer.

When constructing large or complex rules, it is often wise to apply optimization (section 4.1) to the resulting automata.

5.2.3 RULE COMPILATION IN PYNINI

The Pynini `cdrewrite` function is used to compile context-dependent rewrite rules into WF-STs. The first four arguments, all mandatory, include a transducer defining τ, unweighted acceptors defining the left and right environments L and R—an empty string is used for null environments—and a cyclic, unweighted acceptor representing Σ^*, the closure over the rule's alphabet. The reserved symbol [BOS] ("beginning of string") can be used to symbolize the left boundary symbol ^ when constructing L; similarly, [EOS] ("end of string") can be used to symbolize the right boundary symbol $ when constructing R. The optional keyword argument `mode` allows one to specify directionality of application; left-to-right application is the default. Some example snippets are given below.

- Compile rule (3) for simultaneous application:

```
rule = pynini.cdrewrite(
    pynini.cross("b", "a"),
    "b",
    "b",
    pynini.union("a", "b", "c").closure(),
```

```
        direction="sim"
    )
```

- Compile rule (8) for left-to-right application:

```
rule = pynini.cdrewrite(
    pynini.cross("b", "a"),
    "[BOS]b",
    "b",
    pynini.union("a", "b", "c").closure()
)
```

5.3 RULE APPLICATION

At first glance, applying a rule to a string may seem as simple as composing the input string with the rewrite rule transducer and then extracting the output string. However, there are several complexities which may arise when the rule transducers, or the composition of the input string and rule, are cyclic, non-deterministic, and/or weighted. Advanced procedures for rewrite rule application are described below.

5.3.1 LATTICE CONSTRUCTION

The first step in rule application is the creation of a **lattice** of output strings. First, one composes the input acceptor with the rule transducer, possibly taking advantage of implicit conversion from strings to acceptors. If the string is not in the domain of the rule, this will result in an empty automaton, and one may wish to check for this case before continuing.

```
lattice = string @ rule
assert lattice.start() != pynini.NO_STATE_ID
```

Then, to convert this automaton from a transducer to an acceptor over output strings, one simply computes the output projection, optionally applying ϵ-removal afterward. Both operations can be applied in-place.

```
lattice.project("output").rmepsilon()
```

5.3.2 STRING EXTRACTION

There are several different ways to extract output strings from the lattice. If the rule provides only one output string—or if the rule transducer is deterministic—then there will be at most one output path. Similarly, if one wishes to extract only the shortest path from a lattice which may contain multiple paths, one can first call the shortestpath function. One can then simply call the string method to retrieve the output string, as shown below.

```
ostring = pynini.shortestpath(lattice).string()
```

If multiple strings are desired, one can simply extract all output strings using the path iterator so long as the lattice is acyclic. However, a non-deterministic lattice may be ambiguous (section 4.1), meaning that there are multiple paths generating an output string. To avoid this, one may wish to determinize the lattice before extracting strings. However, as discussed in section 4.1, not all weighted non-deterministic automata (NFAs) are determinizable, and even for those which are determinizable, the algorithm may produce a deterministic automaton (DFA) which is exponentially larger than the equivalent NFA.[8] If one needs only the n shortest paths, then Pynini's shortestpath function with unique=True, will perform just as much determinization as is required to find the n shortest paths. This will generate an acyclic, determistic, ϵ-free acceptor, from which one can retrieve the output strings. This is illustrated in the snippet below.

```
lattice = pynini.shortestpath(lattice, nshortest=n, unique=True)
ostrings = list(lattice.paths().ostrings())
```

Alternatively, one may be interested in retrieving all rewrites. In this case, to forestall the possibility of exponential blowup, one can approximate the full deterministic automaton using **pruned determinization** (Rybach et al. 2017). This algorithm computes a DFA approximating the NFA while preferring shorter paths as measured by path weight. The user must specify a state threshold—an upper bound for the size of the determinstic FSA—a weight threshold— a lower bound for the weights of paths in the approximation—or both. In practice, pruned determinization with a state threshold that is some small multiple of the number of states in the non-deterministic FSA (e.g., 4) plus a small constant factor (e.g., 256) yields an exactly-equivalent deterministic FSA for the vast majority of real-world cases, while eliminating the risk of exponential blowup. This is illustrated below.

```
state_threshold = 4 * lattice.num_states() + 256
lattice = pynini.determinize(lattice, nstate=state_threshold)
ostrings = list(lattice.paths().ostrings())
```

Another form of pruned determinization can be used to detect whether there are ties for the single shortest path and to avoid implementation-defined tie resolution. One can apply pruned determinization with a weight threshold of $\bar{1}$, which gives an acyclic, deterministic, ϵ-free acceptor containing all optimal paths, i.e., paths whose weight is the same as that of the single shortest path. This form of pruning is shown in the following snippet.

```
one = pynini.Weight.one(lattice.weight_type())
lattice = pynini.determinize(lattice, weight=one)
```

---

[8]For example, Hopcroft et al. (2008:§2.3.6) describe a class of NFAs with $n + 1$ states for which the equivalent DFA must have at least 2^n states. However, such cases are rare in practice.

If the resulting DFA contains multiple paths, a tie for the single shortest path is present. One can then extract all optimal paths from the DFA using a path iterator, as shown in the following snippet.

```
ostrings = list(lattice.paths().ostrings())
```

Note, however, that the shortest path and pruned determinization algorithms are well defined only over path semirings (subsection 1.5.1).

5.3.3   REWRITING LIBRARIES

The `rewrite` module, part of Pynini's extended library (Appendix C), automates the rewriting procedures described above. It defines several functions which take an input string (or automaton) and a rule transducer, construct the output lattice, and return either a single output string or a list thereof.

1. `rewrites` returns all output strings in an arbitrary order.

2. `top_rewrites` returns the n shortest-path output strings in an arbitrary order.

3. `top_rewrite` returns the shortest-path output string using implementation-defined tie resolution.

4. `one_top_rewrite` returns the single shortest-path output string, raising an exception if there is a tie for the single shortest path.

5. `optimal_rewrites` returns all output strings which have the same weight as the single shortest path in an arbitrary order.

The `rewrite` module also defines the `matches` function, which tests if a rule transducer ζ matches an input-output string pair. A rule ζ matches input x to output y if the intersection $\pi_o(x \circ \zeta) \cap y$ is non-null.

5.4   RULE INTERACTION

There are various mechanisms one can use to combine rewrite rules. These are described below.

5.4.1   TWO-LEVEL RULES

Influential early work by Koskenniemi (1983) proposes a **two-level** model of rule interaction. This approach is, in the authors' opinion, quite obsolete, but is still useful to motivate more sophisticated forms of rule interaction. In the two-level model, each rewrite rule is an assertion about relations between the substrings of the relation the rule governs, i.e., it expresses a constraint on the relation. For instance, Koskenniemi's **composite rules** state that for symbols $s, t \in \Sigma$ the input s must correspond to t in all environments defined by L and R. Two-level rules must be **surface-true** in the sense that they must express exceptionless generalizations about the relationship between input and output substrings. By definition, then, surface-true rules do not interact, and can be combined into a single transducer using an algorithm that is functionally equivalent to intersection (Roark and Sproat 2007:105f.).

As an example, consider the following generalizations regarding the pronunciation of *c* in Latin American dialects of Spanish.

1. *c* is read as [s] when followed by *i* or *e* (e.g., *cima* /sima/ 'summit').

2. *c* is read as [k] elsewhere (e.g., *escudo* /eskudo/ 'shield').

The following surface-true composite rules formalize these generalizations.

(13) $\{c\} \times \{s\} / \underline{\quad} \{i, e\}$

(14) $\{c\} \times \{k\} / \underline{\quad} (\Sigma - \{i, e\})$

Note that while the prose description refers to the reading of *c* as /k/ as the "elsewhere" case, the two-level model requires one to explicitly define the right-context regular language to avoid overlap with other rules. While this is not particularly difficult here, the surface-true restriction can quickly become onerous when working with large, complex collections of rewrite rules. That said, we note that work in the two-level tradition has continued, and there have been many refinements and improvements to the formalism, for example Yli-Jyrä and Koskenniemi 2006, Koskenniemi and Silfverberg 2010, Drobac et al. 2012 and Yli-Jyrä 2013.

5.4.2   CASCADING

The most common alternative to the two-level approach described above is **cascading** or **chaining**, in which rules are applied in a fixed, user-specified order, with the output of one rule fed as input to the next. While a cascade can include surface-true rules, which will apply independently of any other rule, an earlier rule may also—in the terminology of Kiparsky (1968)—**feed**—i.e., trigger, or create the environment for—or **bleed**—block, or eliminate the environment for—a later rule in the course of derivation. By loosening the requirement that rules be surface-true, one can simplify the rules governing Spanish *c*. Consider the rule below.

(15) $\{c\} \times \{k\} / \underline{\quad}$

Unlike earlier rules, this rule is not surface-true: a *c* followed by *i* or *e* does not correspond to surface [k]. However, if one applies (15) to the output of rule (13), this problem is eliminated. In other words, (15) is applied after earlier rules have eliminated any exceptions and therefore can apply "across the board". This is schematicized below.

	cima	*escudo*	orthographic form
(16)	sima		(13)
		eskudo	(15)
	sima	eskudo	phonemic form

There are two ways to implement cascading of a sequence of rewrite rules. In the first method, one simply loops over the rules in specified order. On the first iteration of the loop, one constructs a lattice following the method described in subsection 5.3.1. On subsequent iterations, the lattice from the previous iteration is used as input for the next rule in the cascade, and another lattice is constructed. An example function illustrating this logic is shown below.

```
def cascade(istring: pynini.FstLike,
            rules: Iterable[pynini.Fst]) -> pynini.Fst:
    lattice = istring
    for rule in rules:
        lattice @= rule
        assert lattice.start() != pynini.NO_STATE_ID
        lattice.project("output").rmepsilon()
    return lattice
```

Then, one can extract strings from the output lattice using the methods introduced above in subsection 5.3.2. A complete implementation of this procedure is provided by the Pynini extended library module `rule_cascade`; its `RuleCascade` class generalizes the `rewrite` functions to rule cascades.

However, it is also straightforward to combine a sequence of context-dependent rewrite rules into a single transducer. Since weighted finite transducers are closed under composition, one can create a single rule implementing the cascade by composing the rules in the order in which they are to be applied, optionally optimizing the resulting transducer. For instance, a cascade of the rule sequence [r1, r2, r3] is equivalent to simple rule application with the transducer r1 @ r2 @ r3. Composition and optimization of a rule cascade may be computationally expensive, particularly when the constituent rules are complex or when Σ is large. One generally prefers the loop-based cascading described earlier when an automaton produced by composing multiple rules would be prohibitively large.

5.4.3   EXCLUSION

Occasionally one may wish to apply a sequence of rules so that the successful application of an earlier rule blocks application of any and all later rules, a form of interaction known as **exclusion**. Exclusion is applicable when a series of rules are in competition, and are specified so that they may fail to apply to certain input strings. For instance, one may wish to compose an irregular rule so that it applies to a subset of possible inputs, pre-empting application a general rule that can apply to any string in Σ^*. As an example, consider the orthographic form of English noun plurals. Most plurals are formed by appending an -s to the singular form, but there are a number of exceptions. First, there are "zero" plurals like *deer*, stem-change plurals such as *feet* and *mice*, irregularly suffixed plurals as in *oxen*, plurals with *f-v* alternations as in *wolves*, and Greco-Latin plurals like *nuclei*. The following expression constructs a transducer mapping between singular and plural forms for nouns with irregular plurals.

```
irregular = pynini.string_map(
    [
        "deer",
        "fish",
        "sheep",
        ("foot", "feet"),
        ("mouse", "mice"),
        ("child", "children"),
        ("ox", "oxen"),
        ("wife", "wives"),
        ("wolf", "wolves"),
        ("analysis", "analyses"),
        ("nucleus", "nuclei"),
        ...
    ]
)
```

Only three other rules are required to handle the vast majority of noun plurals. But first, one must define the relevant inventories, including lowercase orthographic vowels (v), consonants (c), and the closure of their union (sigma_star).

```
v = pynini.union("a", "e", "i", "o", "u")
c = pynini.union(
    "b", "c", "d", "f", "g", "h", "j", "k", "l", "m", "n",
    "p", "q", "r", "s", "t", "v", "w", "x", "y", "z"
)
sigma_star = pynini.union(v, c).closure().optimize()
```

One rule converts a final -*y* to -*ies* when -*y* is immediately preceded by a consonant, as in *puppies*, but not when the -*y* is preceded by a vowel, as in *boys*.

```
ies = sigma_star + c + pynini.cross("y", "ies")
```

Another rule appends -*es* to stems ending in -*s*, -*sh*, -*ch*, -*x*, and -*z* as in *churches* or *faxes*. For this one can use the insert function from the pynutil module, part of Pynini's extended library (see Appendix C). Given an acceptor representing the regular language A, insert constructs a transducer representing the rational relation $\emptyset \times A = \{(\epsilon, a\} \mid a \in A\}$.[9]

```
sibilant = pynini.union("s", "sh", "ch", "x", "z")
es = sigma_star + sibilant + pynutil.insert("es")
```

The third and final rule simply appends an -*s*. It imposes no conditions on application other than the requirement that the input be a substring of Σ^*.

```
s = sigma_star + pynutil.insert("s")
```

It should be clear that this last rule is not surface-true. But at the same time one cannot obtain the expected result with cascading either; a cascade of the four rules would produce the erroneous *wolvesess.

There are two ways to apply these rules so that successful application of an earlier rule excludes subsequent rules. One method simply uses a loop to apply each rule in user-specified order. If at any point rule application succeeds—i.e., produces a non-empty lattice—this lattice is returned. Otherwise, the next rule in the list is applied to the input string. An example function implementing this procedure is provided below.

```
def exclude(istring: pynini.FstLike,
            rules: Iterable[pynini.Fst]) -> Optional[pynini.Fst]:
    for rule in rules:
        lattice = istring @ rule
        if lattice.start() == pynini.NO_STATE_ID:
            continue
        return lattice.project("output").rmepsilon()
```

However, it is also possible to combine all rules into a single transducer and still obtain the desired exclusion logic. The **priority union** (Kaplan 1987, Karttunen 1998) of two rational relations μ and ν is similar to their union except that the first relation takes precedence over the second. For instance, suppose that μ transduces string a to b, and ν transduces a to c. Then whereas $\mu \cup \nu$—their union—maps a to both b and c, their priority union gives precedent to μ, and thus only maps a onto b. Formally, priority union can be defined in terms of elementary operations over rational relations. Intuitively, the priority union requires one to filter from ν those relations which are governed by μ. Assuming that $\pi_i(\mu)$ is a subset of Σ^*, $\overline{\pi_i(\mu)}$, the complement of the domain of μ, is given by the regular language $\Sigma^* - \pi_i(\mu)$. Then, the priority union of μ and ν is written

$$\mu \cup_p \nu = \mu \cup \left(\overline{\pi_i(\mu)} \circ \nu \right)$$

[9]The pyutil module also defines a delete function which constructs a transducer implementing $A \times \emptyset = \{(a, \epsilon) \mid a \in A\}$.

where $\cup_p$ is the priority union operator. At the automaton level, priority union is well defined so long as $\pi_i(\mu)$ is determinizable, as it will be so long as it is unweighted. An example function implementing this logic is provided below.

```
def priority_union(mu: pynini.Fst, nu: pynini.Fst,
                   sigma_star: pynini.Fst) -> pynini.Fst:
    nu_not_mu = (sigma_star - pynini.project(mu, "input")) @ nu
    return mu | nu_not_mu
```

To construct the compound plural rule, one repeatedly applies this function, and then optionally optimizes the result, as in the following snippet.

```
rule = priority_union(
    irregular,
    priority_union(ies,
                   priority_union(es, s, sigma_star),
                   sigma_star),
    sigma_star,
).optimize()
```

The `plurals` module, part of Pynini's `examples` library (Appendix D), contains the above implementation of the pluralization rules. The interested reader might improve this module by adding to the list of irregulars or by exploiting other subregularities in the system.

5.5 EXAMPLES

Three applications of rewrite rules are now illustrated.

5.5.1 SPANISH GRAPHEME-TO-PHONEME CONVERSION

Speech technologies like automatic speech recognition and text-to-speech synthesis require mappings between words and their pronunciations. When large, digital pronunciation dictionaries are available, various machine learning techniques can be used to induce these mappings (e.g., Gorman et al. 2020). But for many orthographies, the relation is simple enough that one can simply enumerate the necessary rewrite rules and compile them into a transducer. Spanish is an example of what Rogers (2005) calls a **shallow phonemic orthography**, because there is a near one-to-one relation between characters (**graphemes**) and their pronunciations (**phonemes**). Thus, with a small number of rewrite rules, it is possible to correctly predict the pronunciation of every Spanish word—except for the occasional unassimilated loanword—from its spelling alone. In fact, the rules governing Spanish pronunciation are sufficiently simple that only a few rewrite rules are needed. We now sketch out a grapheme-to-phoneme conversion system that maps Spanish words onto a broad International Phonetic Alphabet (IPA) transcription of their pronunciation, using a cascade of context-dependent rewrite rules.

Let G be the set of graphemes and P the set of phonemes. Then, it is natural to conceive of grapheme-to-phoneme conversion as a function or relation between strings of graphemes in G^*, henceforth written in italics, and phonemes in P^*, henceforth enclosed in square brackets.[10] The snippet below defines these two sets for our sketch of Spanish; note that g and p are not properly disjoint because, for instance, *t* is pronounced [t].

```
g = pynini.union(
    "a", "á", "b", "c", "d", "e", "é", "f", "g", "h", "i", "í",
    "j", "k", "l", "m", "n", "ñ", "o", "ó", "p", "q", "r", "s",
    "t", "u", "ú", "ü", "v", "w", "x", "y", "z"
)
p = pynini.union(
    "a", "b", "d", "e", "f", "g", "i", "j", "k", "l", "ʝ", "m",
    "n", "ɲ", "o", "p", "r", "ɾ", "s", "ʃ", "t", "u", "w", "x", "z"
)
```

Recall, however, that context-dependent rewrite rules compilation requires that all rules be relations over some Σ^*. Therefore, Σ^* is defined to be $(G \cup P)^*$.

```
sigma_star = pynini.union(g, p).closure().optimize()
```

The cascade approach to rule interaction is assumed here. The first rewrite rule pronounces the digraphs *ch*, *ll* and *qu*, handles the readings of *j*, *ñ*, *v*, *x*, and *y*, and removes acute accents. While each of these might be thought of as a logically separate rule, they are all unconditioned, surface-true generalizations and therefore can be expressed as a single rewrite rule.

```
r1 = pynini.cdrewrite(
    pynini.string_map(
        [
            ("ch", "tʃ"),
            ("ll", "ʝ"),
            ("qu", "k"),
            ("j", "x"),
            ("ñ", "ɲ"),
            ("v", "b"),
            ("x", "s"),
            ("y", "ʝ"),
            ("á", "a"),
            ("é", "e"),
            ("í", "i"),
```

---

[10]We use square brackets here because while the output of this grapheme-to-phoneme transducer is broad, we do not wish to make precise claims about the ontological status of these segments in the grammar of Spanish.

```
          ("ó", "o"),
          ("ú", "u"),
          ("ü", "w"),
      ]
  ),
  "",
  "",
  sigma_star,
).optimize()
```

The next rule is a simple one; it deletes *h*, which is normally silent. This rule must be applied after the previous block so that *ch* receives the proper reading. Were the rules applied in the opposite order—or simultaneously, as part of the same rewrite rule—one would not obtain the proper reading for the *ch* digraph.

```
r2 = pynini.cdrewrite(
    pynutil.delete("h"),
    "",
    "",
    sigma_star
).optimize()
```

The third block rewrite rules deals with the pronunciation of *r*. In intervocalic position, Spanish has a contrast between *r*, a flap, as in *pero* 'but', and the trill *rr*, as in *perro* 'dog'. This is addressed using two ordered rules. The first, r3, maps intervocalic *r* to the flap; the second, r4, maps *rr*—which only occurs intervocalically—onto the trill. One can verify that the two rules must be applied in the order specified here to obtain the correct result.

```
v = pynini.union("a", "e", "i", "o", "u")
r3 = pynini.cdrewrite(
    pynini.cross("r", "ɾ"),
    v,
    v,
    sigma_star
).optimize()
r4 = pynini.cdrewrite(
    pynini.cross("rr", "r"), "", "", sigma_star
).optimize()
```

The third and final block of rules deals with the realization of *c* and *g*. The relevant generalizations, repeated in part from earlier, are given below.

1. *c* is read as [s] when followed by *i* or *e*, as in *cima* [sima] 'summit'.

2. *c* is read as [k] in all other positions, as in *escudo* [eskudo] 'shield'.

3. *g* is read as [x] when followed by *i* or *e*, as in *gema* [xema] 'gem'.

4. *g* is read as [g] in all other positions, as in *gato* [gato] 'cat'.

The following rules handle these cases. The first rule, r5, handles the readings of *c* and *g* before the front vowels; the second, r6, maps *c* to /k/ in all other positions; any remaining *g* requires no additional rules.

```
r5 = pynini.cdrewrite(
    pynini.string_map([("c", "s"), ("g", "x")]),
    "",
    pynini.union("i", "e"),
    sigma_star
).optimize()
r6 = pynini.cdrewrite(
    pynini.cross("c", "k"), "", "", sigma_star
).optimize()
```

As defined above, each of the rules operates over a Σ^* containing both graphemes and phonemes. It may be desirable, however, to restrict the input to grapheme sequences and the output to phoneme sequences. Let us suppose that the cascade is represented by the transducer ζ. This filtering can then be affected by $G^* \circ \zeta \circ P^*$—which intersects the domain with G^* and the range with P^*—and optionally optimizing the result, as shown in the following snippet.

```
rules = r1 @ r2 @ r3 @ r4 @ r5 @ r6
g2p = pynini.closure(g) @ rules @ pynini.closure(p)
g2p.optimize()
```

These six rewrite rules, applied as a cascade or composed in order, sketch out a simple grapheme-to-phoneme converter. However, one should note that a few liberties with Spanish pronunciation have been taken:

- It was assumed that *x* is always read /s/ but it may also be read as [ks, x, h] depending on word and dialect.

- The realization of diphthongs such as *ie* [je] and *ue* [we] has not been addressed.

- No attempt has been made to handle stress assignment.

Furthermore, allophonic rules such as the lenition of *d* have been ignored. Such rules are needed to provide a narrow phonetic transcription, which may be useful in certain speech applications. An implementation of the above rules can be found in the g2p module, part of Pynini's `examples` library (Appendix D), and the interested reader might make improvements to address the limitations mentioned above.

5.5.2   FINNISH CASE SUFFIXES

Vowel harmony refers to a phonological process in which the properties of one vowel seemingly assimilate onto another. In some cases, the source and target vowel may be arbitrarily distant, and at first it might seem like this would make it difficult to encode using context-dependent rewrite rules. As shown below, this is not the case.

Finnish exhibits vowel harmony in several contexts, including in the distribution of **locative case suffixes**, which can be likened to English locational prepositions like *in* and *on*. Several of these suffixes, along with their traditional names and glosses, are listed below.

(17)

-tta/-ttä	abessive	'without'
-lta/-ltä	ablative	'off of'
-lla/-llä	adessive	'on'
-sta/-stä	elative	'out of'
-na/-nä	essive	'as a'
-ssa/-ssä	inessive	'in'

Each of the above suffixes above has two **allomorphs** (i.e., variants): one ending in *a* and one in *ä*. Their distribution is determined by the vowels of the adjective or noun to which they are attached. The back vowels—including *a*, *o*, and *u*—select the *a*-allomorph. The front rounded vowels—including *ä*, *ö*, and *y*—select the *ä*-allomorph. In the case that the stem contains both back and front round vowels, the harmonic vowel closest to the suffix governs harmony. Consonants and all other vowels are ignored for the purpose of harmony. Finally, the *ä*-allomorph is the default, used for those stems which contain neither back nor front rounded vowels. Several adessive case examples—some from Ringen and Heinämäki (1999)—are given below, with the harmony-governing stem vowel in bold.

(18)

ver**o**lla	'tax'
g**a**stilla	'sailor'
kes**y**llä	'tame'
k**ä**dellä	'hand'
v**e**ljellä	'brother'
v**e**killä	'pleat'

In his finite-state phonology of Finnish, Koskenniemi (1983:76f.) assumes that the harmonic suffixes contain an **archiphonemic** or **underspecified** vowel which is neither front or nor back. A series of surface-true rules map this archiphonemic vowel, written *A*, onto *a* or *ä*. It is somewhat easier yet to encode the harmony pattern using a cascade of two rewrite rules: the first maps *A* to *a* in the presence of a back-harmonic stem vowel, and the second maps remaining instances of *A* to *ä*. To implement this cascade of rules, one must first define the relevant segmental inventories, including the three classes of vowels.

```
back = pynini.union("a", "o", "u")
front = pynini.union("ä", "ö", "y")
neutral = pynini.union("e", "i")
v = pynini.union(back, front, neutral, "A")
c = pynini.union(
    "b", "c", "d", "f", "g", "h", "j", "k", "l", "m",
    "n", "p", "q", "r", "s", "t", "v", "w", "x", "z"
)
sigma_star = pynini.union(v, c).closure()
```

One can then use these to define the two harmony rules, which are composed and jointly optimized. In the first rule, the left context corresponds to an infinite language BN^* where B is the set of back-harmonic vowels and N the set of neutral segments; the second rule applies across the board.

```
harmony = (
    pynini.cdrewrite(
        pynini.cross("A", "a"),
        back + pynini.union(neutral, c).closure(),
        "",
        sigma_star
    ) @
    pynini.cdrewrite(
        pynini.cross("A", "ä"), "", "", sigma_star
    )
).optimize()
```

Given an input with the archiphonemic A, the cascade defined above applies the appropriate harmony pattern, as shown in the following snippet.

```
assert rewrite.one_top_rewrite("verollA", harmony) == "verolla"
assert rewrite.one_top_rewrite("kesyllA", harmony) == "kesyllä"
```

However, for some applications—such as morphological generation, the subject of the following chapter—it may be desirable to use this rule to help construct various inflectional forms of Finnish words. For instance, one could define a function which takes as input the citation form (the nominative singular) and generates the appropriate adessive form.

```
def adessive(cf: str) -> str:
    return rewrite.one_top_rewrite(cf + "llA", harmony)
```

An implementation of Finnish locative suffixes along these lines can be found in the case module, part of Pynini's examples library (Appendix D).

5.5.3 CURRENCY EXPRESSION TAGGING

Speech technologies like automatic speech recognition (ASR) and text-to-speech synthesis (TTS) often demand another type of mapping between written and spoken language. Speech recognizers and synthesizers usually operate over the "spoken domain", containing entities like *twelve pounds*, but not equivalent "written domain" expressions like *£12*, and speech systems which process or generate written-domain text (e.g., Pusateri et al. 2017, Shugrina 2010) must be able to map between the two domains. Sproat et al. (2001) refer to this process as **text normalization**, and Taylor (2009) refers to entities that require normalization—numbers, dates and times, currency, and measure expressions, abbreviations, etc.—as **semiotic classes**. Text normalization has traditionally been performed using finite-state transducers (e.g., Sproat 1996) although there have been many attempts to exploit machine learning for this task (see Zhang et al. 2019 for a recent review). Google's Kestrel text normalization engine, described in detail by Ebden and Sproat (2014), processes written-domain text in two stages. During the initial "tokenization and classification" stage, the various semiotic classes are identified in the text. Then, in the "verbalization" stage, semiotic class-specific finite-state transducer grammars are applied to each semiotic class span, producing spoken-domain text. The example here is a fragment of the tokenization and classification stage; the more challenging process of verbalization is illustrated in section 7.3.

Suppose one wishes to construct a finite-state transducer which is capable of "tagging" English currency expressions like *$4.59*, *€.80*, or *¥1400*. Such a transducer can naturally be expressed as an unconditioned context-dependent rewrite rule which matches any currency expression, inserting XML-style tags around the expression. Assume that such expressions consist of a currency symbol (e.g., *$*) or followed by either a sequence of Arabic digits (e.g., *140*) or a decimal to two places (e.g., *4.59*, *.80*). For simplicity, delimiters—like commas—used to group numbers are ignored. One begins by building acceptors that match the components of a currency expression so defined. First, the currency symbol acceptor matches the symbol for the dollar, euro, pound sterling, and yen, and can easily be expanded to handle other symbols.

```
cur_symbol = pynini.union("$", "€", "£", "¥")
```

The numeric portion of the expression is matched by `cur_numeric` below. This is defined using the constant `DIGIT` defined by the `byte` module, part of Pynini's extended library (Appendix C), which matches any one Arabic digit. This is used to define acceptors matching the "major" and "minor" portions of a currency expression.

```
major = byte.DIGIT ** (0, ...)
minor = byte.DIGIT ** (2, ...)
cur_numeric = major + ("." + minor) ** (0, 1)
```

We then concatenate the two expressions, producing an acceptor matching written currency expressions.

```
cur_exp = cur_symbol + cur_numeric
```

To turn this into a tagger automaton, we define τ, a transducer which matches the currency expression and inserts the XML-style tags. We then compile τ into a context-dependent rewrite rule using the closure over the vocabulary (here, bytes) as Σ^*, so that non-currency expression text is passed through unadulterated. This is illustrated in the following snippet.

```
tagger = pynini.cdrewrite(
    pynutil.insert("<cur>") + cur_exp + pynutil.insert("</cur>"),
    "",
    "",
    byte.BYTE ** (0, ...)
).optimize()
```

One can then use `tagger` to rewrite written-domain text with currency tags. However, this tagger automaton has many ambiguities. Consider for instance the input I have £50. One might expect this to be tagged I have <cur>£50</cur>, but the tagger defined above also permits I have <cur>£5</cur>0, in which the final 0 is left out of the expression. Let us assume that one would prefer a "greedy" tagging, in which the tags enclose the longest possible sequence.[11] One way to enforce this is to assign a negative weight to each Arabic digit matched, and then compute the shortest path output string, which will necessarily be the one with the longest possible sequence. Using `add_weight`, another helper function from the `pynutil` module, one can attach a weight to an FST. In the snippet below, this function is used to redefine the numeric components of the currency matcher.

```
major = pynutil.add_weight(byte.DIGIT, -1) ** (0, ...)
minor = pynutil.add_weight(byte.DIGIT, -1) ** (2, ...)
```

If these alternative weighted definitions are used to build `cur_exp` and `tagger` as above, then the shortest-path output string produced by applying the rule using `one_top_rewrite` will be greedy in the relevant sense.

The `tagger` module, part of Pynini's extended library (Appendix C), automates the construction and application of general-purpose tagger automata.

FURTHER READING

Bale and Reiss (2018) provide a detailed introduction to the SPE rule notation, conventions for rule application, phonological features, and natural classes.

Three of the early proponents of context-dependent rewrite rules—Ronald Kaplan, Lauri Karttunen, and Martin Kay—are recipients of the Association for Computational Linguistics'

---

[11]We note that it is not strictly necessary to use weights to achieve a greedy match. This can also be handled using, e.g., **directed replacement** (Karttunen 1996).

prestigious Lifetime Achievement Award, and all three discuss the import of this technology in the published transcriptions of their acceptance speeches (Kaplan 2019, Karttunen 2007, Kay 2005).

There have been a number of further refinements to rule compilation procedures since Kaplan and Kay 1994 and Mohri and Sproat 1996. See, for example Hetherington 2001, Skut et al. 2003, Yli-Jyrä and Koskenniemi 2006, Yli-Jyrä 2007, and Drobac et al. 2012.

Roark and Sproat (2007: ch. 4) review Koskenniemi's two-level model and its equivalence to rational relations.

Sproat (2000) argues that the process of grapheme-to-phoneme conversion can be described by a rational relation for all known writing systems; Ebden and Sproat (2014) make a similar claim for text normalization. Recent work by Jane Chandlee and colleagues, reviewed by Heinz (2018) and discussed in section 8.3 below, argues that nearly all known phonological and morphological processes are **subsequential functions** and can be implemented by deterministic finite-state transducers.

We have put aside the representation of tone and other prosodic-metrical phenomena; see Yli-Jyrä 2013 for some recent work on this topic.

CHAPTER 6

Morphological Analysis and Generation

The previous chapter included several examples in which rewrite rules were used to generate variants—including plurals and locative case forms—of various words. Building on these techniques, this chapter provides a systematic finite-state treatment of **morphology**, the study of word formation and word-internal structure.

Much of the early work in speech and language processing treated words—however defined—as indivisible units of linguistic meaning, and as such ignored the relationship between English words like *lock*, *locked*, *locksmiths*, *padlock*, and *unlockable*. Modeling these relations soon became necessary, however. Early work in **information retrieval** (effectively, early versions of search engines) found it helpful to reduce sparsity by conflating related English words using **stemmers**, cascades of handwritten, language-specific suffix-stripping rules (e.g., Porter 1980). The "stems" produced need not even be real words—for instance, applying the Porter stemmer to some of the previous text yields non-words like *cascad*, *languag*, and *produc*—so long as words sharing the same stem fall into semantically coherent equivalence classes. Intuitively, someone who searches the internet or a database for *fishing* may also be interested in documents that only mention *fish*. Replacing words with their "stems" allows retrieval systems to improve generalization and reduce the computing and memory requirements of indexing and retrieval. At roughly the same time, early word processing and typesetting systems were forced to model morphology to compress large lists of words—for spell-checking (McIlroy 1982) and hyphenation (Liang 1983), for example—to fit within limited random access memory of the era's microcomputers.[1] One of the more systematic early computational treatments of English morphology was undertaken by the developers of MITalk, a **text-to-speech synthesis** engine. This system is described by Allen et al. (1987) and Klatt (1987), although work began almost two decades earlier.[2] MITalk includes a module called DECOMP which decomposes complex words into their constituent parts for the purposes of predicting their pronunciations. DECOMP consists of a list of stems and **affixes** (e.g., prefixes and suffixes), and rules governing the spelling of complex words. For example, consider the word *scarcity*, which is composed of *scarce* plus *-ity*, a suf-

---

[1]As an apocryphal story has it, Bill Gates told the audience of a 1980s trade show that 640 kilobytes of memory "ought to be enough for anybody". For comparison, the roughly 235,000 headwords of the second edition of *Webster's New International Dictionary* (Neilson and Knott 1934) constitute 2.2 MB of ASCII text.

[2]DECTalk, a commercial variant of MITalk put out by the Digital Equipment Corporation, is best known as the adopted voice of late physicist and author Stephen Hawking.

fix forming abstract nouns from adjectives. DECOMP generates this word—and thus recovers its decomposition—by concatenating *scarce* and *–ity* and applying a spelling rule that deletes a word-final *e* before certain suffixes; such rules are available only at the right edge of a stem. At the same time, DECOMP considers, but rejects, an alternative analysis *scar-city* (which, for instance, might refer to an urban area where scars are a common sight). This decomposition would yield an incorrect pronunciation, and various hand-tuned heuristics are used to avoid such incorrect decompositions. The system is able to generate over 100,000 words from its 12,000 lexical entries (Klatt 1987:773).

To the modern reader, the data and memory limitations motivating early work on morphological analysis may seem as distant as the 1980s themselves, but such problems still resonate today. Modern laptops may have several orders of magnitude more memory than the microcomputers used to run MITalk, but text processing systems are also expected to run on mobile devices, including affordable cellular phones, with limited computational resources.

6.1   APPLICATIONS

Many systems that process or generate speech or text may need to be sensitive to morphology. For example, the following chapter (section 7.6) illustrates the generation of weather reports. For English, such a system might use a template like `It's $TEMP degrees and $CONDITIONS in $LOCATION`. While this would correctly generate expressions like `It's twelve degrees and cloudy in Montreal`, it also would produce the ungrammatical *`one degrees`` on certain cold days. **Internationalization** of text generation or processing systems originally built for English—or Mandarin—may require a great deal of morphological sophistication, simply because these languages have an uncommonly impoverished morphology. Whereas in English, a noun inflects for **number** (e.g., *one city*, *two cities*), Russian nouns are also inflected for **case**, which indicates the noun's grammatical function in the clause. As Russian has six cases and two numbers, a noun's **paradigm**—its list of inflected forms—may have as many as twelve variants. In practice, although, many forms may appear in multiple **slots** or **cells** in the paradigm, a phenomenon known as **syncretism**. The paradigm of a Russian noun is shown in Table 6.1 below; note the syncretism between nominative and accusative forms is characteristic of inanimate nouns.[3] Russian poses a somewhat greater challenge for the weather generation example above, for one says *odín grádus* 'one degree', *trí grádusa* 'three degrees', and *vósem' grádusov* 'eight degrees', using the nominative singular, genitive singular, and genitive plural forms, respectively.

The above example is an instance of **morphological generation**, and models which perform it are known as **generators** or **inflectors**. In this scenario, one wishes to produce a certain form of a stem, for example, the instrumental plural form of the Russian word *žurnál* 'magazine, journal', having already determined the appropriate form to use in this context. De-

---

[3] Russian examples have been transliterated from their Cyrillic spellings. Primary stress, marked here with an acute accent, is not part of the standard Cyrillic orthography of Russian, but is indicated here.

Table 6.1: Paradigm for the Russian masculine noun *grádus* 'degree'.

	Singular	Plural
Nominative	grádus	grádusy
Genitive	grádusa	grádusov
Dative	grádusy	grádusam
Accusative	grádus	grádusy
Instrumental	grádusom	grádusami
Prepositional	gráduse	grádusax

termining the proper morphological form to use in a given context is beyond the scope of this chapter. The inverse procedure, **morphological analysis**, recovers the **citation form** or **lemma**—roughly, the form one would expect to find this word listed under in a dictionary—and the **morphosyntactic features** of an inflected form. For instance, *žurnálami* is analyzed as the instrumental plural of *žurnál* 'magazine, journal', and might be represented by the string žurnál+ami[num=pl][case=ins] where the boundary symbol '+' separates stems and affixes and the morphosyntactic features are written in square brackets. In some cases, one is not as interested in morphosyntactic features of the inflected word but simply wishes to recover its lemma, a process referred to as **lemmatization**. Conversely, some applications of morphosyntactic features do not require a decomposition into stem and affixes, a scenario referred to as **morphological tagging**. When applied to documents, morphological analysis may require one to first segment the text stream into sentences and/or words. **Sentence splitting** and **tokenization** also lie beyond the scope of this book, and may be non-trivial for certain scripts, particularly certain scripts of East Asia which do not consistently delimit word boundaries with whitespace or punctuation.

Lemmas and morphosyntactic features are commonly used to provide features to **part-of-speech tagging** (e.g., Denis and Sagot 2009, Hajič 2000, Halácsy et al. 2006) or **syntactic parsing** (e.g., Dehouck and Denis 2018, Dubey 2005, Fraser et al. 2013) systems, particularly in richly inflected languages. Lemmas are also used as a sophisticated alternative to stemming in information retrieval applications.

Computational morphological analysis and generation, including most of the examples in this chapter, often makes use of orthographic inputs and outputs rather than phonemic representations. There are several reasons for this. First, most applications of of morphological analysis or generation naturally take in or and/or produce orthographic forms, so additional effort is required to phonemic representations internally. Second, orthographic representations have little effect in languages like Finnish or Spanish, which have shallow, highly consistent orthographies that are quite close to phonemic or phonetic transcriptions. In contrast, languages like English and Korean have what Rogers (2005), inter alia, calls **deep orthographies**, meaning that spellings are more abstract. In English spelling, one rarely indicates morphologically conditioned changes in vowel quality, and as a result, related words like *sane* and *sanity* are spelled quite similarly despite the fact that they have different stem vowels (Chomsky and Halle 1968:44f.). One is therefore free to ignore stress shift and vowel reduction processes in English when building an orthographically based morphological analyzer.

6.2   WORD FORMATION

There are many different theoretical frameworks used by linguists studying morphology. One major distinction, is between the family of **item-and-arrangement** theories, which analyze a word like *žurnálami* as the concatenation of two meaningful **morphemes**—e.g., the stem *žurnál* and the instrumental plural suffix **-ami**—and **item-and-process** theories which views affixation as just one type of transformation applied to a base (Hockett 1954). However, Karttunen (2003) and Roark and Sproat (2007: ch. 3) argue that this distinction—as well as the additional distinction between **lexical** and **realizational** theories popularized by Stump (2001)—are essentially computationally equivalent because all the relevant processes under either family of theories are largely equivalent to the rational relations and can be modeled by cascades of finite-state transducers. Furthermore, FSTs designed for generation can be modified for analysis, lemmatization, or tagging depending on one's needs.

Koskenniemi's broad-coverage morphology of Finnish, reviewed in detail by Roark and Sproat (2007: ch. 4), was one of the first attempts to use finite-state automata for morphological analysis and generation. The model Koskenniemi proposed became something of a standard for fieldwork and language documentation of morphologically rich languages (Antworth 1990). The subsequent discovery of algorithms for compiling rewrite rules (chapter 5) in the 1980's, greatly simplifies the process of constructing an analyzer, inflector, lemmatizer, or tagger. Using the tools already discussed, there are numerous ways one might build a finite-state analyzer. Indeed, this "many ways to do it" freedom is one of the more pleasant features of finite-state computing. Perhaps the simplest approach for dealing with Russian nouns, for example, would be to simply construct a transducer from wordforms to their associated features; it would be straightforward to convert this analyzer to a inflector, lemmatizer, or tagger. This is illustrated in the snippet below. If this resulting transducer is called ν, then given μ, an FST mapping from features to human-readable strings, one could extract the analyses of a string s from the lattice $\pi_o(s \circ \nu \circ \mu)$.

```
nouns = pynini.string_map(
    [
        ("žurnál", "žurnál+[num=sg][case=nom]"),
        ("žurnála", "žurnál+a[num=sg][case=gen]"),
        ("žurnálu", "žurnál+u[num=sg][case=dat]"),
        ("žurnál", "žurnál+[num=sg][case=acc]"),
        ("žurnálom", "žurnál+om[num=sg][case=ins]"),
```

```
    ("žurnále",  "žurnál+e[num=sg][case=prp]"),
    ("žurnálá",  "žurnál+y[num=pl][case=nom]"),
    ("žurnálóv", "žurnál+ov[num=pl][case=gen]"),
    ("žurnálám", "žurnál+am[num=pl][case=dat]"),
    ("žurnálá",  "žurnál+y[num=pl][case=acc]"),
    ("žurnáláx", "žurnál+ax[num=pl][case=prp]"),
    ("žurnálámi","žurnál+ami[num=pl][case=ins]"),
  ]
)
```

Of course, to cover a sizeable chunk of Russian noun morphology would require adding whatever nouns one wanted to cover. The disadvantages of this approach should be clear: the list of forms would be need to be extremely large to obtain broad coverage. While this approach is workable, it is not ideal. One would prefer a method that allows one to

1. share information across multiple stems in the same paradigm,

2. inherit information from related paradigms,

3. conveniently represent morphosyntactic features and feature bundles, and

4. construct analyzers, generators, lemmatizers, and taggers.

The remainder of this chapter introduces the `features` and `paradigms` modules, part of Pynini's extended library (Appendix C), which provide precisely this functionality.

6.3   FEATURES

While the term has a much broader sense in morphological theory, here a **feature** refers to morphosyntactic property that defines the slots within a given paradigm. For instance, Russian noun paradigms are defined by case and number. Classes in the `features` module can be used to define features and slots. The first argument to the `Feature` constructor is the name of the feature, and the remaining arguments define the names of valid values for that feature. Case and number features are defined in the following snippet.

```
case = features.Feature(
    "case", "nom", "gen", "dat", "acc", "ins", "prp"
)
num = features.Feature("num", "sg", "pl")
```

A `Category` is a combination of features, expressed as an acceptor which accepts any sequence of the feature-value pairs it is constructed from. Thus, the noun `Category` defined in the following snippet will admit feature combinations like {[case=nom], [num=sg]}, or {[case=ins], [num=pl]}.

```
noun = features.Category(case, num)
```

Finally, a `FeatureVector` represents a valid combination of a `Category` and a sequence of feature specifications. For instance, the following combinations are valid.

```
nomsg = features.FeatureVector(noun, "case=nom", "num=sg")
genpl = features.FeatureVector(noun, "case=gen", "num=pl")
inspl = features.FeatureVector(noun, "num=pl", "case=ins")
```

6.4   PARADIGMS

Having defined the slots in a paradigm, it now is necessary to combine them into a paradigm. This is accomplished using the `paradigms` module. One first selects a boundary symbol to separate wordforms into stems and affixes, conventionally '+'. The function `make_byte_star_except_boundary` is used to construct a definition of a stem, here $(\Sigma - \{+\})^*$ where Σ is the set of bytes.

The `paradigms` module follows Roark and Sproat (2007: ch. 2)—and the spirit of the item-and-process model—in that affixes are introduced via composition rather than concatenation. Thus, a suffix s permitted to attach to any stem corresponds to the rational relation $\zeta = S(\emptyset \times \{s\})$, where S is the set of stems. Then, then $\pi_o[x \circ \zeta]$ where $x \in S$, corresponds to the string xs, and a similar logic applies for prefixes. This may seem like a roundabout way of defining affixation, but it—unlike concatenation—is general enough to allow for additional restrictions on stem shape, to permit the affix to trigger a change to the stem, or even to permit the affix to insert itself into the stem, all of which are seen in the following examples.

6.5   EXAMPLES

The remainder of this chapter sketches morphological analyzers for four languages. We focus here on cases that involve relatively complex paradigmatic relationships, or non-concatenative systems where the affixation is sensitive to the phonological shape of the base. Of course purely concatenative and potentially unbounded morphology of the kind as discussed by Hankamer (1989) for Turkish (see section 5.1) is also important, but then again it is more obvious how one might implement such cases. We leave it as an exercise for the reader to implement a model that can handle examples like *marginalizationalizationalizátion* discussed in section 5.1.

6.5.1   RUSSIAN NOUNS

In the `paradigms` module, a paradigm is primarily defined by slots, and each slot is defined by a pair consisting of an affixation transducer and a `FeatureVector`. For Russian nouns, since the relevant affixes are suffixes that impose minimal constraints on their stems, these affixation transducers are defined using the module's `suffix` function, which constructs a simple suffixation relation ζ given stem shape and suffix acceptors; a `prefix` function is also provided.

A `Paradigm` is constructed from

1. the `Category`,

2. a list of slots, and

3. a `FeatureVector` defining the lemma,

4. a list of stems (strings or acceptors),

as well as several optional fields illustrated below. The `Paradigm` can then lazily construct ana-lyzer, tagger, lemmatizer, and inflector transducers. The following snippets implement the so-called "hard stem masculine accent A", which includes Russian nouns like *grádus* and *žurnál*, using the nominal features and noun category defined above. Note that the lemma is assumed to be the nominative singular form. This is shown in the following snippets.

- Defines the stem shape:

```
stem = paradigms.make_byte_star_except_boundary()
```

- Defines the slots:

```
slots = [
    (stem, nomsg),
    (paradigms.suffix("+a", stem),
     features.FeatureVector(noun, "case=gen", "num=sg")),
    (paradigms.suffix("+u", stem),
     features.FeatureVector(noun, "case=dat", "num=sg")),
    (stem,
     features.FeatureVector(noun, "case=acc", "num=sg")),
    (paradigms.suffix("+om", stem),
     features.FeatureVector(noun, "case=ins", "num=sg")),
    (paradigms.suffix("+e", stem),
     features.FeatureVector(noun, "case=prp", "num=sg")),
    (paradigms.suffix("+y", stem),
     features.FeatureVector(noun, "case=nom", "num=pl")),
    (paradigms.suffix("+ov", stem),
     features.FeatureVector(noun, "case=gen", "num=pl")),
    (paradigms.suffix("+am", stem),
     features.FeatureVector(noun, "case=dat", "num=pl")),
    (paradigms.suffix("+y", stem),
     features.FeatureVector(noun, "case=acc", "num=pl")),
    (paradigms.suffix("+ami", stem),
     features.FeatureVector(noun, "case=ins", "num=pl")),
```

```
        (paradigms.suffix("+ax", stem),
         features.FeatureVector(noun, "case=prp", "num=pl")),
    ]
```

- Constructs the paradigm:

```
masc_accent_a = paradigms.Paradigm(
    category=noun,
    name="hard stem masculine accent A",
    slots=slots,
    lemma_feature_vector=nomsg,
    stems=["grádus", "žurnál"]
)
```

The "hard stem masculine accent B" paradigm can be similarly defined. The only difference between this and the accent A paradigm is that word stress shifts to the suffix in all cases except the nominative and accusative singular, a process which be traced back thousands of years to the accentual system of Proto-Indo-European (Halle 1997). Thus, for instance, the dative singular of *górb* 'hump, hunch' is *gorbú* and the nominative plural of *stól* 'table' is *stolý*. To generate this pattern, one needs only to place an acute accent on the appropriate vowel in the suffix, and then to provide a rule deaccenting the stem. Note also that Σ^* for this rule must include the output features, obtained from the output projection of the noun Category's feature mapper automaton. The optional parent_paradigm argument to Paradigm allows this to inherit any slots not redefined from another paradigm, here, nominative and accusative singular forms from the accent A paradigm. Finally, the optional rules argument specifies an optional list of rules—here, just the deaccentuation rule—to be applied when constructing wordforms. The following snippets demonstrate the construction of the accent B paradigm. Note that the noun object provides Σ^* for the rewrite rule.

- Defines the deaccentuation rule:

```
deaccentuation_map = pynini.string_map(
    [
        ("á", "a"), ("é", "e"), ("í", "i"),
        ("ó", "o"), ("ú", "u"), ("ý", "y"),
    ]
)
acc_v = pynini.project(deaccentuation_map, "input")
deaccentuation = pynini.cdrewrite(
    deaccentuation_map, "", noun.sigma_star + acc_v, noun.sigma_star
).optimize()
```

- Defines the slots:

```
slots = [
    (paradigms.suffix("+á", stem),
     features.FeatureVector(noun, "case=gen", "num=sg")),
    (paradigms.suffix("+ú", stem),
     features.FeatureVector(noun, "case=dat", "num=sg")),
    (paradigms.suffix("+óm", stem),
     features.FeatureVector(noun, "case=ins", "num=sg")),
    (paradigms.suffix("+é", stem),
     features.FeatureVector(noun, "case=prp", "num=sg")),
    (paradigms.suffix("+ý", stem),
     features.FeatureVector(noun, "case=nom", "num=pl")),
    (paradigms.suffix("+óv", stem),
     features.FeatureVector(noun, "case=gen", "num=pl")),
    (paradigms.suffix("+ám", stem),
     features.FeatureVector(noun, "case=dat", "num=pl")),
    (paradigms.suffix("+ý", stem),
     features.FeatureVector(noun, "case=acc", "num=pl")),
    (paradigms.suffix("+ámi", stem),
     features.FeatureVector(noun, "case=ins", "num=pl")),
    (paradigms.suffix("+áx", stem),
     features.FeatureVector(noun, "case=prp", "num=pl")),
]
```

- Defines the paradigm:

```
masc_accent_b = paradigms.Paradigm(
    category=noun,
    name="hard stem masculine accent B",
    slots=slots,
    parent_paradigm=masc_accent_a,
    lemma_feature_vector=nomsg,
    stems=["górb", "stól"],
    rules=[deaccentuation]
)
```

To demonstrate the use of the two paradigms, consider the following function, which prints all the forms of a given stem using the stem_to_forms transducer to generate the wordform itself, and the feature_label_rewriter transducer to produce a human-readable representation of the feature vector.

```
def print_forms(noun: str, pd: paradigms.Paradigm) -> None:
    lattice = rewrite.rewrite_lattice(
```

```
        noun,
        pd.stems_to_forms @ pd.feature_label_rewriter
    )
    for wordform in rewrite.lattice_to_strings(lattice):
        print(wordform)
```

The following interactive session shows the outputs for *grádus* and *stól*.

```
>>> print_forms("grádus", masc_accent_a)
grádus+ami[case=ins][num=pl]
grádus+am[case=dat][num=pl]
grádus+ax[case=prp][num=pl]
grádus+a[case=gen][num=sg]
grádus+e[case=prp][num=sg]
grádus+om[case=ins][num=sg]
grádus+ov[case=gen][num=pl]
grádus+u[case=dat][num=sg]
grádus+y[case=nom][num=pl]
grádus+y[case=acc][num=pl]
grádus[case=nom][num=sg]
grádus[case=acc][num=sg]
>>> print_forms("stól", masc_accent_b)
stol+ý[case=acc][num=pl]
stol+ý[case=nom][num=pl]
stol+ú[case=dat][num=sg]
stol+óv[case=gen][num=pl]
stol+óm[case=ins][num=sg]
stol+é[case=prp][num=sg]
stol+á[case=gen][num=sg]
stol+áx[case=prp][num=pl]
stol+ám[case=dat][num=pl]
stol+ámi[case=ins][num=pl]
stól[case=acc][num=sg]
stól[case=nom][num=sg]
```

6.5.2 TAGALOG INFIXATION

Consider an example where affixation is not merely concatenative. Like many other Austronesian languages, Tagalog, spoken in the Philippines, makes use of **infixes**, affixes which attach to the middle of stems. To form the actor-focus infinitive form, one inserts *-um-* between a word-initial consonant C and the following vowel V, or initially—i.e., as a prefix—if there is

Table 6.2: Tagalog *um*-infixation, after Ramos and Bautista (1986).

Lemma	Actor Focus (-um-)	
bilang	**bum**ilang	'count'
ibig	**um**ibig	'love'
kopya	**kum**opya	'copy'
lipad	**lum**ipad	'fly'
punta	**pum**unta	'go to'

no word-initial consonant. Some examples are given in Table 6.2, and the following snippets implement Tagalog *um*-infixation.

- Constructs the focus feature, the verb category, and the lemma feature vector:[4]

```
focus = features.Feature("focus", "none", "actor")
verb = features.Category(focus)
none = features.FeatureVector(verb, "focus=none")
```

- Defines V, C and the stem shape:

```
v = pynini.union("a", "e", "i", "o", "u")
c = pynini.union(
    "b", "d", "f", "g", "h", "k", "l", "ly", "k", "m", "n",
    "ng", "ny", "p", "r", "s", "t", "ts", "w", "y", "z"
)
stem = paradigms.make_byte_star_except_boundary()
```

- Defines *um*-infixation as stem-form rule:

```
um = pynini.union(
    c.plus + pynutil.insert("+um+") + v + stem,
    pynutil.insert("um+") + v + stem
)
```

- Defines the slots:

```
slots = [
    (stem, none),
    (um, features.FeatureVector(verb, "focus=actor")),
]
```

[4]While omitted here, there are several other types of focus in Tagalog.

- Constructs the paradigm:

```
tagalog = paradigms.Paradigm(
    category=verb,
    slots=slots,
    lemma_feature_vector=none,
    stems=["bilang", "ibig", "lipad", "kopya", "punta"],
)
```

The following interactive session shows the outputs for *bilang* and *ibig*.

```
>>> print_forms("bilang", tagalog)
bilang[focus=none]
b+um+ilang[focus=actor]
>>> print_forms("ibig", tagalog)
ibig[focus=none]
um+ibig[focus=actor]
```

6.5.3   YOWLUMNE ASPECT

An even more complex example comes from Yowlumne (formerly Yawelmani), an endangered language spoken in California. This particular example comes to us from Newman (1944) via Archangeli (1984).[5] In this language, verbal aspect is expressed via suffixation with concomitant reshaping of the verb stem. These shapes can be described in terms of **templates** of vowels and consonants, and thus Yowlumne provides a novel example of **templatic morphology** not dissimilar to better-known examples like Arabic and Hebrew.

Four aspectual suffixes can attach to the verb root: dubitative *-al*, passive aorist *-t*, gerundial *-inay*, and durative *-aa*.[6] The first two suffixes are said to be "neutral" because, unlike the latter two, they do not trigger any stem changes. However, the gerundial, for example, is associated with a template represented by the regular language $CVCC^?$ where C is the set of consonants and V the set of vowels. This does not trigger any changes to *caw* 'shout', because it is a subset of $CVCC^?$, but with the stem *hoyoo* 'name', the gerundial stem is realized as *hoy*, with truncation of the final long vowel. Similarly, the durative is associated with a $CVCVVC^?$ template, where the doubled V indicates a long vowel. Thus, the stems *caw* and *ilk* 'sing' have durative stems *cawaa-* and *ʔiliik-*, respectively. Additional examples are provided in Table 6.3.

Archangeli (1984) describes the conventions necessary to map stems onto templates, but what matters here is that these mappings are also regular relations. The transducers implementing these templates may either insert or delete material, and the paradigm slots are defined

---

[5] Blevins (2004) and Weigel (2005) note that much of the Yowlumne data used by Archangeli and others consist of hypothetical words posited by earlier authors—particularly Kuroda (1967)—on the basis of rules and stems provided by Newman (1944). Therefore, these particular data should be taken with a grain of salt.

[6] In these transcriptions ʔ represents the glottal stop, *c* a voiceless alveolar affricate. Long vowels are indicated by doubled vowels.

Table 6.3: Yowlumne aspectual suffixes, after Archangeli (1984:252). Note that the *-n* suffix after the durative ending *-ʔaa* is a tense suffix: see Newman (1944:97).

Lemma	-al	-t	-inay	-ʔaa(-n)	
caw	cawal	cawt	cawinay	cawaaʔaa-n	'shout'
cuum	cuumal	cuumt	cuminay	cumuuʔaa-n	'destroy'
hoyoo	hoyooal	hoyoot	hoyinay	hoyooʔaa-n	'name'
diiyl	diiylal	diiylt	diylinay	diyiilʔaa-n	'guard'
ʔilk	ʔilkal	ʔilkt	ʔilkinay	ʔiliikʔaa-n	'sing'
hiwiit	hiwiital	hiwiitt	hiwtinay	hiwiitʔaa-n	'walk'

by inserting the appropriate suffixes and composing the stem with the appropriate affix. The $CVCVVC^{?}$ template requires one to copy certain vowels to indicate lengthening. Generally speaking, string relations that copy arbitrary unbounded sequences are not rational relations, but one can simulate this effect using an iterated union over the eligible segments. The following snippets implement the Yowlumne aspectual system as a paradigm.

- Constructs the aspect feature, the verb category, and the lemma feature vector:

```
aspect = features.Feature(
    "aspect", "root", "dubitative", "gerundial", "durative"
)
verb = features.Category(aspect)
root = features.FeatureVector(verb, "aspect=root")
```

- Defines C, V, and the stem shape:

```
c = pynini.union(
    "c", "m", "h", "l", "y", "k", "ʔ", "d", "n", "w", "t"
)
v = pynini.union("a", "i", "o", "u")
stem = paradigms.make_byte_star_except_boundary()
```

- Defines the $CVCC^{?}$ template for *-inay*:

```
cvcc = (
    c + v + pynutil.delete(v).ques +
    c + pynutil.delete(v).star + c.ques
).optimize()
```

- Defines the $CVCVVC^?$ template for $-?aa$:

```
cvcvvc = pynini.Fst()
for vowel in ["a", "i", "o", "u"]:
    cvcvvc.union(
        c + vowel + pynutil.delete(vowel).ques +
        c + pynutil.delete(vowel).star +
        pynutil.insert(vowel + vowel) + c.ques
    )
cvcvvc.optimize()
```

- Defines the slots:

```
slots = [
    (stem, root),
    (paradigms.suffix("+al", stem),
     features.FeatureVector(verb, "aspect=dubitative")),
    (paradigms.suffix("+inay", stem @ cvcc),
     features.FeatureVector(verb, "aspect=gerundial")),
    (paradigms.suffix("+?aa", stem @ cvcvvc),
     features.FeatureVector(verb, "aspect=durative")),
]
```

- Constructs the paradigm:

```
yowlumne = paradigms.Paradigm(
    category=verb,
    slots=slots,
    lemma_feature_vector=root,
    stems=["caw", "cuum", "hoyoo", "diiyl", "?ilk", "hiwiit"]
)
```

The following interactive session shows the outputs for *caw* and *ilk*.

```
>>> print_forms("caw", yowlumne)
caw[aspect=root]
cawaa+?aa[aspect=durative]
caw+inay[aspect=gerundial]
caw+al[aspect=dubitative]
>>> print_forms("?ilk", yowlumne)
?ilk[aspect=root]
?iliik+?aa[aspect=durative]
```

Table 6.4: Examples of Latin lemmas and stems for three conjugations.

	Lemma	1st Stem	2nd Stem	3rd Stem	
1st conj.	laudō	laud-	laudāv-	laudāt-	'praise'
2nd conj.	moneō	mon-	monu-	monit-	'warn'
3rd conj.	agō	ag-	ēg-	act-	'drive'

```
?ilk+inay[aspect=gerundial]
?ilk+al[aspect=dubitative]
```

6.5.4   LATIN VERBS

Finally, the Pynini distribution includes a fairly extensive treatment of over 2,500 Latin verbs from three conjugations. Salient properties of Latin verbs include agreement with the subject's **person** (first, second, or third) and **number** (singular or plural), **active** and **passive** voices for most verbs, and three separate stems. Roughly speaking, the first stem is used for present, future and imperfect forms, and the present participle, the second stem for perfect aspectual forms, and the third stem for participial forms and various productive nominalizations. Examples of these stems are given in Table 6.4. In all cases it is assumed that the citation form, the first person singular active indicative present, is the lemma.

The relation between the stems of the first conjugation is largely regular in that most verbs of this conjugation exhibit a pattern similar to that of *laud-*, the second and particularly third conjugations are much more irregular. Some of the most complex patterns include **reduplication** (e.g., the second stem of *spondeō* 'promise' is *spopond-*) and **suppletion**, the use of phonologically dissimilar stems within a single paradigm (e.g., the second and third stems of *ferō* 'bring' are *tul-* and *lāt-*, respectively). However, it is notable that no matter the shape of a given stem, that stem is used in the same contexts across all verbs; for example, there are no exceptions to the generalization that passive participles and nominalizations in *-iō* are built from the third stem. While there are some subregularities, the third stem of a verb is not fully predictable from the verb's other stems, and there do not seem to be any particular syntactic or semantic commonalities between the various uses of the three stems. Aronoff (1994) refers to morphological generalizations that are phonologically, syntactically, and semantically arbitrary—like the Latin third stem—as **morphomic**.

FURTHER READING

Aronoff and Fudemann (2011) provide an accessible introduction to the theory of morphology. Sproat (1992) describes the early history of computational morphology.

Many of the computational issues and examples discussed in this chapter are addressed in greater detail by Roark and Sproat (2007); their Chapter 2 reviews many examples of morphological processes, including fragments of Latin, Tagalog, and Yowlumne, Chapter 3 argues that item-and-arrangement and item-and-process theories are computationally equivalent, and Chapter 5 reviews machine learning approaches to morphology up to that date.

Kurimo et al. (2010) reviews the Morpho Challenge shared tasks on unsupervised morphological learning, held 2005–2010. More recently, the Conference on Natural Language Learning (CoNLL) and the ACL Special Interest Group on Computational Morphology and Phonology (SIGMORPHON) have hosted a series of shared tasks on supervised morphological analysis and generation (Cotterell et al. 2016, 2017, 2018, McCarthy et al. 2019, Vylomova et al. 2020). Beemer et al. (2020) use the results of the 2020 SIGMORPHON shared task to compare "hand-written" morphological analyzers to ones based on neural networks.

CHAPTER 7

Text Generation and Processing

This chapter presents several finite-state text generation and processing applications. These include fuzzy string matching, text normalization and disambiguation, and text generation. Many of the applications here, as well as the morphological analysis examples in the previous chapter, can be thought of as instances of the **noisy-channel model**. In a noisy channel model, the goal is to recover an original "signal" of some sort after it has been corrupted by "noise". To do this, one constructs a model of the noise—in the form of a transducer—and then attempts to find the most likely signal using shortest-path decoding.

7.1   FUZZY STRING MATCHING

Fuzzy (or **approximate**) **string matching** refers to techniques used to find strings similar to some query string. Applications include plagiarism detection, spelling correction, and computer-aided translation. One tool for fuzzy matching is the **edit transducer**, a weighted automaton, usually over the tropical semiring, with domain and range Σ^* for which identity mappings are "free" (i.e., have weight $\bar{1}$). Given an edit transducer η and input and output strings $x, y \in \Sigma^*$, paths through the lattice $x \circ \eta \circ y$ represent weighted alignments from x to y. Each transition in η represents one of the following operations:

1. a **match** between two identical symbols c_x, c_y where $c_x = c_y$: $\{c_x\} \times \{c_y\}$,

2. the **insertion** of an output symbol not present in the input: $\emptyset \times \{c_y\}$,

3. the **deletion** of an input symbol not present in the output: $\{c_x\} \times \emptyset$, and

4. the **substitution** of an input symbol c_x for an output symbol c_y where $c_x \neq c_y$: $\{c_x\} \times \{c_y\}$.

Then, then one can construct η via the closure of an automaton in which each of these operations is denoted by an arc. An example of this construction is shown in Figure 7.1. To see how the edit transducer produces an alignment between input and output strings, consider the lattice fragment in Figure 7.2. Each path through this lattice is a possible alignment; for instance, the path $[0, 2, 3, 4, 8, 9]$ could be schematicized

```
_abba
bab_a
```

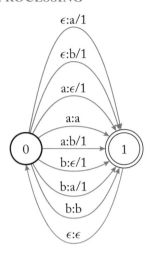

Figure 7.1: Simple edit transducer η over $\Sigma = \{a, b\}$; the match operation is free whereas insertion, deletion, and substitution each have cost 1.

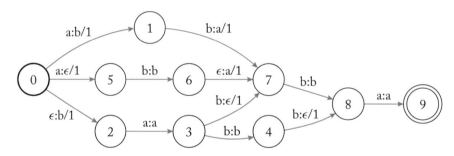

Figure 7.2: Fragment of the lattice $\{abba\} \circ \eta \circ \{baba\}$, with suboptimal paths pruned. Each path through the lattice defines an alignment between abba and baba.

where underscores indicate insertion or deletion.

This naïve construction of an edit transducer requires $s^2 + 2s + 1$ arcs where $s = |\Sigma|$ is the size of the alphabet. Unfortunately, this quadratic growth factor results in very large automata for all but the smallest alphabets. For example, more than 9,000 arcs are required when Σ is the 95 printable ASCII characters. To avoid this blowup, in many cases one may split the edit transducer into two factors η_x, η_y such that $\eta_x \circ \eta_y$ is isomorphic to η and $(x \circ \eta_x) \circ (\eta_y \circ y)$ is isomorphic to $x \circ \eta \circ y$. These two factors treat each edit as a two-part process. In the case of substitution, for example, the η_x factor maps each input symbol onto a reserved symbol [sub] representing substitution—$\Sigma \times \{[sub]\}$—and the η_y factor performs the inverse mapping $\{[sub]\} \times \Sigma$. The resulting factors exhibit linear growth rate in the size of the alphabet and

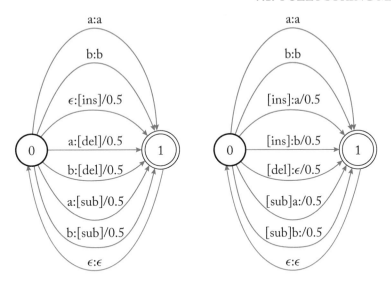

Figure 7.3: Left (η_x) and right (η_y) factors of the edit transducer over $\Sigma = \{a, b\}$.

thus are feasible even for large alphabets. An example of the two edit transducer factors is given in Figure 7.3.

Edit distance or **Levenshtein distance** (Levenshtein 1966) is a widely used measure of string similarity according to which the distance between two strings x, y is defined by the minimum number of insertions, deletions, and substitutions needed to transduce from x to y. While there exist many special-purpose algorithms for computing edit distance (e.g., Wagner and Fischer 1974), it can be trivially computed for a pair of strings x, y using an edit transducer: it is simply the total shortest distance (section 4.2) through $x \circ \eta \circ y$ or the factored variant $(x \circ \eta_x) \circ (\eta_y \circ y)$. In fact, one can generalize edit distance to virtually any set of non-negative costs so long as

1. matches are free,

2. non-matches have cost $> \bar{1}$, and

3. the cost of substitution is less than the cost of insertion plus the cost of deletion.

Now imagine that one wishes to find the string or strings in some lexicon $L \subseteq \Sigma^*$ that are most similar to a query string $q \in \Sigma^*$ according to some generalized edit distance η represented by factors η_x, η_y. Naïvely, one could simply compute the edit distance between the query and each word in the lexicon, although such an approach would be quite expensive given a large lexicon. Instead, one can match q against $\eta \circ L$, a **Levenshtein automaton** (Schulz and Mihov 2002). The n shortest paths through $\pi_o(q \circ \eta \circ L)$—or equivalently, through $\pi_o((q \circ \eta_x) \circ (\eta_y \circ$

L))—represent the n closest matches to q in L, Note also that the right-hand term $L' = \eta_y \circ L$ can be computed offline, as in the following snippet.

```
lprime = eta_y @ pynini.string_map(
    [
        "caithness",
        "camembert",
        "cheshire",
        "gouda",
        "gruyere",
        "roquefort",
    ]
)
```

The following snippet illustrates searching the Levenshtein automaton for the nearest match. Note that the output projection can remain implicit in this case, because the `string` method ignores input labels.

```
lattice = "rockford" @ eta_x @ lprime
lattice.project("output").rmepsilon()
assert pynini.shortestpath(lattice).string() == "roquefort"
```

The `edit_transducer` module, part of Pynini's extended library (Appendix C), automates the construction and use of edit transducers and Levenshtein automata.

Searching a Levenshtein automaton with cyclic edit transducers can be quite slow. Therefore, one can, following Schulz and Mihov (2002), approximate η by building edit transducers (or their factors) which permit no more than k non-match operations. When the alphabet is large and k is small, this approximation results in much faster searches.

7.2 DATE TAGGING

One of the most frequent semiotic classes, introduced in subsection 5.5.3, are dates. There are many ways to write a given calendar date; for example, *October 20th*, *Oct. 20th*, and *10/20* are all common American English renderings of the same date, and the day-month orders like *20/10* are also found throughout the Anglophone world. In a TTS system, one needs to convert expressions like *10/20* to a spoken-domain expression like *October twentieth*. Similarly, the language model component of ASR systems are commonly trained on large corpora of written text in which dates are only rarely written as they are spoken. In addition to speech applications, the equivalences between various ways of writing a date are useful for **information retrieval** and **information extraction** systems like search engine indexers. Consider the following paragraph:[1]

---

[1]Source: https://en.wikipedia.org/wiki/Winston_Churchill, accessed November 8, 2019.

Churchill was born at the family's ancestral home, Blenheim Palace in Oxfordshire, on **30 November 1874**, at which time the United Kingdom was the dominant world power. Direct descendants of the Dukes of Marlborough, his family were among the highest levels of the British aristocracy, and thus he was born into the country's governing elite. His paternal grandfather, John Spencer-Churchill, 7th Duke of Marlborough, had been a Member of Parliament (MP) for ten years, a member of the Conservative Party who served in the government of Prime Minister Benjamin Disraeli. His own father, Lord Randolph Churchill, had been elected Conservative MP for Woodstock in 1873. His mother, Jennie Churchill (née Jerome), was from an American family whose substantial wealth derived from finance. The couple had met in **August 1873**, and were engaged three days later, marrying at the British Embassy in Paris in **April 1874**. The couple lived beyond their income and were frequently in debt; according to the biographer Sebastian Haffner, the family were "rich by normal standards but poor by those of the rich".

Let us assume that one has a grammar FST called `DATE_MATCHER`, which tags the date expressions written in bold above, isolating months, dates, and years, eliminating ordinal suffixes like the `th` in `4th`, and converting month names like `November` to integers like `11`. Then, by applying `DATE_MATCHER` to the above text and extracting the shortest path's output string, one obtains substrings such as the following.

```
...on <date><day>30</day><month>11</month><year>1874</year></date>...
...in <date><month>8</month><year>1873</year></date>...
...in <date><month>4</month><year>1874</year></date>...
```

Note that the single year `1873` is not tagged by the grammar. This is a deliberate decision because it is hard to determine whether a given four-digit number is a year or simply a cardinal number. Thus, date taggers often avoid solitary years—or limit them to a reasonably narrow range—to avoid overgeneration (e.g., Yarowsky 1997:167).

The `dates` module, part of Pynini's `examples` library (Appendix D), contains a finite-state grammar with behavior as described above. The interested reader might extend this grammar to recognize year-only dates within some sensible range.

7.3   NUMBER NAMING

Numbers are often the first semiotic class to receive attention in a text normalization system. Without a way to read numbers, one cannot read dates, times, currency expressions, measure phrases, and so forth. In a TTS or ASR system, one needs to convert expressions like *3:45* to *three forty five*, and to do this, one must first know how to read *3* and *45*. Digit sequences—additionally including symbols like a comma marking larger powers of ten or a period separating the integral and decimal spans—can express a number of different types of entries. They may include ordinary cardinal numbers such as *three hundred forty two*, decimal numbers like *three point four two*, or be read as a digit sequence (e.g., *three forty two* in a street address or *three four two* as telephone number area code). The first category, ordinary numbers, are the most basic, because one can derive the other categories from them, and are therefore the focus here.[2]

Sproat (1996) reduces the number naming process to two subproblems, namely

1. **factorization** of a digit string into sums of products of powers of ten, and

2. **verbalization** of the components of the factorization.

For 342, the string is factored as $3 \times 10^2 + 4 \times 10^1 + 2$. Then a lexicon mapping from 3 to three, 10^2 to hundred, 4×10^1 to forty, and 2 to 2 suffices to verbalize these factors. This lexicon λ is clearly a rational relation, and with some effort, one can also construct a rational relation ϕ performing factorization up to some suitable quantity (e.g., billions or trillions). Then, the entire number name grammar reduces roughly to the application of a transducer $\phi \circ \lambda^*$. In practice, such a grammar may need some additional rules. For instance, some varieties of English insert *and* between certain components of complex number names (e.g., *three hundred and one*), and in other languages, the verbalization is modified by phrasal phonology. Russian and several other Slavic languages pose a particular challenge: they require certain case, number, and/or gender forms within a complex number name, and concord with the case and number of any nominal expressions modified (Sproat 2010b). However, none of these details change the fundamental nature of the problem.

The numbers module, part of Pynini's example library (Appendix D), includes a simple grammar of ordinary English number names from 1–10 million. The interested reader might extend this grammar by

1. increasing the coverage of the grammar to a higher power (e.g., 10^9),

2. adding a rule to insert *and* as per British English usage,

3. modifying it to generate ordinal numbers like *three hundred forty second*, or

4. developing a number name grammar along similar lines for another language.

7.4   CHATSPEAK NORMALIZATION

Digital textual communication via chat rooms, mobile messaging services like SMS, and social media applications has introduced novel abbreviations—expressions like cul8r 'see you later' and ngl 'not gonna lie'—expressive spellings like cooollll, and new ways to express affective and paralinguistic content, including **emoticons**, **emoji**, and **kaomoji**. Internet language practices— and specifically **chatspeak**, the informal language found in chatrooms, texts, and posts on social

---

[2]English also has special mechanism for reading years: e.g., *1984* is usually read *nineteen eighty four* rather as *one thousand nine hundred eighty four*. In many other languages, years are read as ordinary numbers.

media services—frequently conveys more information than a simple translation into a more formal register can capture. Thus, `cu8lr` suggests certain attitudes and stances than can easily be captured in a simple translation. Similarly, spellings like `coooolll` attempt to represent a previously unwritable prosodic feature, expressive lengthening, that might imply that something is really, really cool, or perhaps a little bit square. Despite these issues, there has been quite a bit of research on automatic normalization of chatspeak using machine learning (e.g., Aw and Lee 2012, Baldwin et al. 2015, Beaufort et al. 2010, Choudhury et al. 2007, Chrupała 2014, Liu et al. 2012, Roark and Sproat 2014, Yang and Eisenstein 2013).

The `chatspeak` and `chatspeak_model` modules, part of Pynini's examples library (Appendix D), implement a simple chatspeak normalization application. The `chatspeak` module consists of four normalization systems, including

1. deduplication, as in `coooollllll` → `cool`,

2. expansion of abbreviations involving the deletion of vowels or sonorant consonants, as in `mnstr` 'monster',

3. a collection of regular expression patterns, such as the spelling of `congratulations` as `congrats`, `congratzz`, `congratzzz`, and so on, and

4. a lexicon mapping from common chatspeak terms to their standard forms.

The system assumes tokenized text and produces a "sausage" lattice such that each token can either be read as it appears or mapped onto zero or more possible normalizations. Most of the code for the chatspeak engine should be self-explanatory. The deduplicator is constructed by composing a set of FSTs, each one of which deduplicates a different letter; this design, similar in spirit to Yowlumne templates (subsection 6.5.3), is unavoidable as there is no straightforward way to express deduplication as a rational relation. A fragment of the chatspeak lexicon is shown in Table 7.1.

To select the appropriate normalization in context, this lattice is scored by intersecting it with a WFSA language model constructed using the OpenGrm-NGram toolkit (Roark et al. 2012), and then decoded by computing the single shortest path. A Bash script for building the language model, `make_chatspeak_lm.sh`, is also included in the Pynini distribution; as set up, it uses a copy of Oscar Wilde's play "The Importance of Being Earnest". Note that some of the normalizations, including deduplication and deabbreviation, require the user to provide a target lexicon. For simplicity, the system builds this lexicon using the vocabulary of the provided language model. The `chatspeak_model` module can be used to intersect and decode lattices produced by the above components with the language model. Some example input-output pairs are shown in Table 7.2. The interested reader might

1. expand the chatspeak grammar by adding new abbreviations or patterns, or

2. build and use a language model from a different corpus that is more appropriate for the chatspeak domain.

Table 7.1: Fragment of the English chatspeak lexicon.

1nam	one in a million
1432	i love you too
abt	about
ack	acknowledgement
afaic	as fast as i can
appt	appointment
apt	appointment
ayt	are you there
b	be
bbiab	be back in a bit
bf	boyfriend
bfn	bye for now
bmt	before my time
bm&y	between me and you
cmon	come on
couldnt've	couldn't have
couldntve	couldn't have
cuz	because
cyt	see you tomorrow
dere	there
dl	download
doesnt	doesn't
dyou	do you
eva	ever
g2g	got to go
gb	goodbye
gfy	good for you
gg	going
gg	good game
gl	good luck
gng	going
goot	good
govt	government
hallo	hello
hand	have a nice day
hth	hope this helps

Table 7.2: Example input-output pairs for the chatspeak-plus-LM model.

1432 earnst	i love you too earnest
the appt is in lndn	the appointment is in london
ily u silly rmntc fooooooolllls	i love you you silly romantic fools

7.5 T9 DISAMBIGUATION

T9 ("text on nine keys") is a predictive text entry system. While originally developed as an assistive technology—i.e., for those who experience difficulties typing on a QWERTY keyboard—it is also used for text entry on "dumbphones" lacking a full keyboard. In the T9 system, the digit keys of a phone are used to type alphabetic text. The 2 key, for instance, is used to type a, b, and c, 3 is used to type d, e, and f, and so on. The 0 key types space, and the 1 key is used for punctuation characters. Clearly, T9 is a rational relation, a subset of $D^* \times A^*$ where $D = \{0, 1, \ldots, 9\}$ and $A = \{a, b, c, \ldots, z, \ldots\}$. The snippet below maps constructs the mapping from numeric keys to lowercase alphabetic symbols and space.

```
t9_map = [
    ("0", [" "]),
    ("2", ["a", "b", "c"]),
    ("3", ["d", "e", "f"]),
    ("4", ["g", "h", "i"]),
    ("5", ["j", "k", "l"]),
    ("6", ["m", "n", "o"]),
    ("7", ["p", "q", "r", "s"]),
    ("8", ["t", "u", "v"]),
    ("9", ["w", "x", "y", "z"]),
]
decoder = pynini.Fst()
for (inp, outs) in t9_map:
    decoder.union(pynini.cross(inp, pynini.union(*outs)))
decoder.closure().optimize()
```

Note that this is a relation, not a function, because an input string like 7378378 can be read as request, pervert, as well as numerous non-words.[3] To filter non-words, one can intersect the decoder's output with an acceptor $L' = L (\{\_\} L)^*$ where L is the union of all dictionary strings and _ represents the space character. Assuming a list of words lexicon, this filter can be constructed using string_map and a utility function from the pyutil module (see Appendix C), as shown below.

---

[3]Words sharing a T9 encoding are sometimes known as **textonyms** (Crystal 2008:68).

Table 7.3: Tabular representation of weather conditions in three cities.

City	Temp. (C)	Wind Speed	Wind Direction	Condition
London	1	5	northwest	cloudy
New York	15	10	southeast	overcast
Tokyo	18	3	south	clear

```
lprime = pynutil.join(pynini.string_map(lexicon), " ")
```

The t9 module, part of Pynini's examples library (Appendix D), implements a simple T9 decoder along the lines described above. The interested reader might

1. extend the T9 grammar to support punctuation symbols, or

2. intersect the output with a language model (which could be a character-level language model), as suggested in the previous section.

7.6   WEATHER REPORT GENERATION

A final application is text generation itself. Traditional approaches to generation (see van Deemter et al. 2005 for an overview) often depend in part on template-filling. Consider the case of generating weather reports, given a tabular representation which gives information such as the temperature, wind speed (in km/h), wind direction, and the general condition, for a set of cities, as shown in Table 7.3. The following is a suitable English template for this representation.

```
In $CITY, it is $TEMPERATURE degrees and $STATE, with winds out of the
$WIND_DIRECTION at $WIND_SPEED kilometers per hour.
```

The weather module, part of Pynini's examples library (Appendix D), demonstrates one way to fill the above template. Data for each city is stored in a Python dictionary. When a weather report is requested for a given city, a transducer mapping between template slots like $CITY or $WIND_SPEED, with each template slot separated by Σ^*. By composing the template with this transducer, one obtains the fully populated weather report. As mentioned in chapter 6, it is necessary to attend to some morphological details, such as number agreement for *degree(s)* and *kilometer(s) per hour*. This is accomplished by treating the plural as the base form and using a transducer to map it to the singular when the preceding quantity is one. In Russian, for instance, one would also need to inflect the city name—e.g., for *v Moskvé* 'in Moscow' for *Moskvá*—which requires additional transducers. The following snippet illustrates the use of the weather generation system.

```
wt = weather.WeatherTable()
wt.add_city("London", 1, 5, "northwest", "cloudy")
```

```
wt.add_city("New York", 15, 10, "southeast", "overcast")
wt.add_city("Tokyo", 18, 3, "south", "clear")
print(wt.generate_report("London"))
```

This prints:

```
In London, it is 1 degree and cloudy with winds out of the northwest at 5
kilometers per hour.
```

This format is preferable for a human reader; to construct input for a TTS system, one could apply the number grammar described above in section 7.3. This is left as an exercise to the interested reader.

FURTHER READING

Mohri (2003) provides a formal analysis of generalized edit distance transducers. Ristad and Yianilos (1998) use expectation maximization to estimate the costs of an edit transducer from parallel data.

The date tagging problem is inspired by Google's Kestrel text normalization system, described in detail by Ebden and Sproat (2014).

Much of what is known about how languages verbalize complex number names can be traced back to Hurford (1975). Power and Longuet-Higgins (1978), Gorman and Sproat (2016), and Ritchie et al. (2019) propose algorithms used to induce finite-state number naming grammars from small samples of data.

Crystal (2006, 2008) and McCulloch (2019) trace the development of chatspeak from early chat rooms to SMS to modern social media applications. Eisenstein (2013) discusses issues in the processing of non-standard internet text.

T9 is just one of many mobile device input methods. Ouyang et al. (2017) describes finite-state methods for decoding text input via on-screen keyboards. Hellsten et al. (2017) generalizes this model to support ad hoc transliterations.

CHAPTER 8

The Future

One may recall from chapter 1 that Kleene introduced the regular languages to study the computational properties of early artificial neural networks. Many decades later, the connection between automata and neural networks may seem no clearer. Finite-state techniques, elegant and well-understood, are a classic example of "neat" artificial intelligence, whereas neural networks are "scruffy"; despite Kleene's efforts, little is known about their expressive capacity, and the heuristics used to train them provide few guarantees. It is no hyperbole to say that we are currently living through a neural network revolution—a "deep learning tsunami" (Manning 2015:701)—that has seen neural networks overtake the world of benchmarks, leaderboards, and shared tasks in speech and language processing. In a world where neural networks have taken over, what role do finite-state transducers have to play?

In our opinion, finite-state methods still play a central role in speech and language technologies and are not going away any time soon. At Google, the OpenFst and OpenGrm libraries remain absolutely essential for latency-sensitive applications like voice search, automated captions in YouTube, and the Google Assistant. Many Google engineers and linguists working on speech and language processing specialize in WFST algorithms or grammar development. While we cannot speak to practices elsewhere in the tech industry, Pusateri et al. (2017) reports that the Apple's Siri assistant uses finite-state grammars—hybridized with a neural network—for **inverse normalization**, i.e., to convert ASR transcripts to a human-readable form. The powerful Kaldi speech recognition toolkit—widely used by academic researchers—uses a WFST decoder, implemented with OpenFst. Other technologies—including modern neural networks—have begun to encroach on the state of the art for speech technologies, and may ultimately render WFSTs obsolete, but such technologies still struggle to compete on latency, particularly for embedded platforms (e.g., mobile devices) lacking the specialized hardware needed to support large neural networks. For instance, at the time of writing the neural network-based text normalization system described by Zhang et al. (2019), which is used to synthesize U.S. English driving directions for Google Maps, nonetheless exceeds the computational capacity of conventional mobile devices.

We believe the future of WFSTs is bright. Below, we review some recent work on finite automata and present a highly speculative prospectus for the future.

8.1   HYBRIDIZATION

One reflection of recent excitement about the potential of neural networks is recent work attempting to hybridize neural and finite automata methods.

One form of hybridization hearkens back to Kleene's early work. Weiss et al. (2018) distill modern neural network language models into an approximately equivalent deterministic finite acceptors, a task known as **extraction**. At present, however, their work is limited to neural language models and thus the automata they extract are acceptors describing languages rather than transducers describing relations. Furthermore, their evaluation is limited to a well-studied collection of toy languages, and it is not clear the proposed method scales.

Reranking is a common technique in speech and language processing, one long predating the current neural network revolution (e.g., Collins and Koo 2005, Shen and Joshi 2005). In a first pass, one uses a simple generative model and the shortest-paths algorithm to generate a lattice of k (perhaps 10–100) unique hypotheses. This generative model might be a finite-state grammar for text normalization, a WFST decoder for speech recognition, a probabilistic context-free grammar for constituency parsing, or a statistical machine translation model. Then, in a second pass, a discriminatively trained model is used to score all paths through the first-pass lattice; the output is the highest-scoring path. In the case that the generative model is probabilistic, the discriminative model can even make use of probabilities computed on the first pass, a special case of **stacked generalization** (Wolpert 1992). This technique exploits the relative strengths of both generative and discriminative methods. Generative models of linguistic sequences are ordinarily **Markovian**: they generate the sequence incrementally using only simple, local features, but support efficient generation of the n shortest paths. In contrast, discriminative models can make use arbitrary features efficiently, but often lack the affordances needed for efficient, exact decoding. Modern neural networks are well-suited to act as the second-pass discriminative model for reranking because embedding, recurrence, and attention layers are powerful representation learners seemingly eliminating the need for painstaking feature engineering.

Since the earliest use of neural networks for language processing, it has been observed that neural models occasionally commit to gross errors that are difficult to explain from first principles. For instance, Pinker and Prince (1988) and Sproat (1992:216f.), reviewing a neural model of English past tense generation (Rumelhart and McClelland 1986), draw attention to bizarre errors such as the prediction of *membled* as the past-tense form of the verb *mail*. Following Gorman and Sproat (2016), we refer to such gross mistakes as **silly errors**. Silly errors are observed in such tasks as machine translation (Arthur et al. 2016), morphological generation (e.g., Corkery et al. 2019, Gorman et al. 2019), and text normalization (e.g., Gorman and Sproat 2016). Sproat and Jaitly (2017) and Zhang et al. (2019) propose neural reranking models for text normalization in which the first pass is effectively a filter performed by an unweighted finite-state **covering grammar**, a highly permissive, one-to-many rational relation which can either be specified by the user or induced from data. For instance, a covering grammar for text normalization might permit an input string like $12 to be read as not just twelve dollars but also `twelve dollar`, `one two dollars`, and so on, but not `eleven euros`. In the second pass, a recurrent neural network scores the paths generated by the first-pass finite state filter. Sproat and Jaitly and Zhang et al. report that this approach substantially reduces silly errors.

Neural networks are often said to be "data-greedy" models requiring large amounts of training data to achieve acceptable performance. **Data augmentation** techniques have commonly been used to improve neural networks' performance in low-resource settings on tasks such as morphological generation (e.g., Bergmanis et al. 2017, Silfverberg et al. 2017) and machine translation (e.g., Fadaee et al. 2017, Li and Specia 2019). Schwartz et al. (2019) and Lane and Bird (2020) use finite-state morphological analyzers for data augmentation: they train neural network morphological analyzers using data sampled from finite-state morphological analyzers.

Another set of hybridization techniques result in models that are simultaneously neural network and finite-state automaton. For example, Rastogi et al. (2016) propose a novel architecture consisting of a finite transducer whose weights are computed using a neural network. The resulting model describes a globally normalized probability distribution over output strings, constrained by the topology of the FST. The network predicts the weight for a given arc using embeddings of the source state and the arcs' input and output symbols, and the contextual encoding of the arc's input symbol produced by a bidirectional recurrent layer scanning the entire input string. They evaluate this model on several morphological generation tasks. Lin et al. (2019) modify Rastogi et al.'s model so that paths, rather than individual arcs, are weighted by a neural network conditioned using arbitrary features of the path, freeing it from the Markovian limitations faced by of earlier hybrid models. They evaluate this model, a **neural finite-state transducer**, on several tasks including grapheme-to-phoneme conversion.

8.2   HARDWARE CUSTOMIZATION

One of the many technologies that enabled the neural network revolution is the wide availability of specialized, power-efficient, parallel, programmable integrated circuits for numerical processing such as **graphics processing units** (GPUs) and **tensor processing units** (TPUs). While custom hardware for graphical rendering have existed for decades, such hardware made the jump to general-purpose computing in 2007 when chip maker Nvidia introduced CUDA, a framework for general-purpose numerical computing on GPUs. Of course, the neural network revolution has been accelerated by many scientific discoveries—refinements of recurrent networks, attention models, novel optimization and regularization techniques, etc.—but it is hard to imagine the rapid scientific progress could have occurred without hardware substantially accelerating training and inference.

Some recent work has tried to accelerate key WFST algorithms—particularly those used for decoding in automatic speech recognition systems—by porting them to GPUs. While this has proved difficult for many WFST algorithms, Argueta and Chiang (2017, 2018) describe parallel, CUDA-based implementations of the FST composition and shortest-path algorithms (respectively), the latter achieving astonishing improvements—when run on a powerful GPU—over a serial, CPU-based implementation. Chen et al. (2018), Fukunaga et al. (2019), and Braun et al. (2020) study the problem of porting the entire decoding process for a WFST-based speech recognition system to GPUs. Should further porting efforts prove infeasible, **application-specific integrated circuits** (ASICs) may be an alternative. It is possible to imagine that embedded devices may someday use custom "WFST chips" for speech generation and processing.

8.3   SUBREGULAR GRAMMAR INDUCTION

Gold (1967) proved that regular languages are in general not "learnable" under the framework of **identification in the limit**. However, there are well-defined subsets—the **subregular languages** and **subregular functions**—and many of these are provably learnable in the sense of Gold (ibid.).

One well-studied family of subregular functions are the **strictly local** (SL) functions (Chandlee et al. 2014). Informally speaking, a function is **input strictly local** (ISL) if for some $k \in \mathbb{N}$, it is possible along each path to predict the output string using no more information than the k preceding input labels. All ISL functions correspond to some deterministic finite transducer, and are provably learned from finite samples of data (e.g., input-output pairs) using a polynomial-time algorithm guaranteed to converge on the target grammar (Chandlee 2014, Jardine et al. 2014). It is known that a wide variety of phonological processes can be modeled with ISL functions or with the closely related **output strictly local** (OSL) functions (Chandlee et al. 2015), and Chandlee (2014) shows that any mapping describable by a simultaneously-applied rewrite rule of the form $\tau \ / \ \lambda \ \_\!\_ \ \rho$ (section 5.1) is ISL so long as the language $\lambda \pi_i(\tau)\rho$ is itself finite.[1] Heinz (2018) suggests that all natural language phonological processes, with the possible exception of total reduplication, are not merely regular functions—as Johnson (1972) observed (section 5.1)—but subregular, subsequential functions including the ISL or OSL families. This contrasts strongly with the scruffy methods used to train neural networks, for which few convergence guarantees and error bounds are known. To our knowledge, demonstrations of subregular grammar induction algorithms have largely been limited to small phonological problems and have not yet been tested at scale. However, one can imagine such algorithms could be used to automatically induce high-quality finite-state grammars from examples, obviating the manual grammar development techniques discussed in chapter 5.

---

[1]It may seem counter-intuitive that ISL functions could model transductions with a non-null right-context ρ. However, the ISL formulation permits null outputs, allowing a rightward-triggered process to "wait" up to k labels. See Heinz 2018:167f. for discussion.

APPENDIX A

Pynini Installation

Pynini can be run on most modern UNIX-like operation systems, including MacOS, Linux, or the Windows Subsystem for Linux (WSL) for Windows 10. For most users, the simplest option is to install the module and its dependencies using Anaconda, a free, multi-platform package management system that includes a recent version of Python 3. However, it is also possible to compile Pynini—and the OpenFst libraries on which it depends—from source. Both installation methods are described below.

A.1 ANACONDA INSTALLATION

1. Install Anaconda, if you have not already. Download the Anaconda Individual Edition installer for your platform, available online.[1] Note that if you are planning on using Pynini on Windows 10, you should download and run the Linux installer (not the Windows installer) using the WSL console. Then, launch the installer and follow all installation instructions.

2. At the command line, issue the following command:

```
conda install -c conda-forge pynini
```

Anaconda can also be used to quickly install current versions of other OpenGrm libraries, including NGram, a command-line library for building finite-state language models. For instance, to install NGram, simply issue the following command:

```
conda install -c conda-forge ngram
```

A.2 SOURCE INSTALLATION

Source installation of Pynini is known to work on MacOS and Linux when

- G++ 4.9 or better, with POSIX, C99, and C++17 support, and

- Python 3.6 or better, with development headers

---

[1]https://www.anaconda.com/products/individual

are available. The instructions given below also assume the user has sudo privileges. Before installing Pynini itself, one must first build and install a compatible version of OpenFst. Note that every version of Pynini is pinned to a specific OpenFst release and is unlikely to compile against earlier or later versions.

1. Download the OpenFst tarball, available online, and note the version number.[2]

2. At the command line, navigate to the directory where the tarball was downloaded, then issue the following command to decompress it, where ${VERSION} is the version number recorded in the previous step:

```
tar -xzf openfst-${VERSION}.tar.gz
```

3. Issue the following command to enter the directory:

```
cd openfst-${VERSION}
```

4. Issue the following commands to configure, build, and install OpenFst:

```
./configure--enable-grm && sudo make -j install
```

This may take several minutes to complete, and at the end of the process, the user may be prompted for their password.

One may then build and install Pynini, as follows.

1. Download the Pynini tarball, available online, and note the version number.[3]

2. At the command line, navigate to the directory where the tarball was downloaded, then issue the following command to decompress it, where ${VERSION} is the version number recorded in the previous step:

```
tar -xzf pynini-${VERSION}.tar.gz
```

3. Issue the following command to enter the directory:

```
cd pynini-${VERSION}
```

4. Issue the following command to build and install Pynini:

```
python setup.py install
```

One can then optionally run the provided unit test by issuing the following command.

```
python tests/pynini_test.py
```

If successful, this will run all tests and print the string OK at the end. Note that some tests intentionally raise warning or error messages; these can be safely ignored so long as the tests themselves pass.

---

[2]http://www.openfst.org
[3]http://pynini.opengrm.org

A.3   OPTIONAL DEPENDENCIES

Graphviz (Ganser and North 2000) is an open-source suite of command-line tools for rendering directed graphs;[4] its dot command is used to generate many figures in this book, and is also compatible with interactive environments like Jupyter notebooks. When installing Pynini via Anaconda, Graphviz is automatically installed as a dependency. However, if one installs Pynini from source, one can also install Graphviz from source or via an appropriate package manager.

---

[4]https://www.graphviz.org/

APPENDIX B

Pynini Bracket Parsing

When compiling strings into transducers in byte and utf8 mode (subsection 2.3.2), unescaped ASCII square bracket characters [and] trigger special processing. The following is the full routine used to parse bracketed spans, i.e., strings enclosed by left and right square brackets.

1. If the bracketed span is empty, an exception is raised.

2. If the bracketed span contains one or more space characters, each space-delimited token is taken to be a **generated symbol**. Each generated symbol is assigned a unique integer label in Unicode Planes 15–16, reserved for private use, and stored in a global symbol table.

3. If the bracketed span does not contain a space, it is processed by the C standard library function stroll, which can parse decimal and hexidecimal integer strings. If this routine succeeds, the integer is used an arc label, but no generated symbols are stored.

4. If none of the above succeed, the entire bracketed span is used as a single generated symbol.

One can later retrieve the table of generated symbols using the generated_symbols function. Generated symbols should be used sparingly since they depend on global state—state that does not persist beyond the interpreter session—and on the order in which expressions are executed. For this reason, they are most appropriate when used as special symbols (e.g., reserved symbols, delimiters) to be discarded at the end of the grammar compilation process. String printing routines do not require any special treatment for either type of square bracket.

To prevent bracket parsing, one can "escape" a square bracket character—causing it to be interpreted as literal bracket character rather than a delimiter for a generated symbol—by inserting a backslash immediately beforehand, as in \[and \]. One can automatically insert escaping backslashes into strings using the Pynini function escape.

APPENDIX C

Pynini Extended Library

The Pynini package includes a collection of additional Python modules, the extended library, distributed in the `pynini.lib` namespace, along with associated unit tests. A brief summary of each module is given below.

- byte: This module contains definitions of finite automata matching ASCII digits (`DIGIT`), alphabetic strings (`ALPHA`), punctuation (`PUNCT`), and so on, similar to the string constants defined in the C standard library header `ctype.h`. These constants can be used to construct the Σ^* automaton used to compile rewrite rules over arbitrary bytestrings. *Nota bene*: these are intended as constants and therefore should not be mutated using destructive methods.

- edit_transducer: This module defines edit transducer and Levenshtein automata classes (section 7.1).

- features: This module defines morphological feature classes (chapter 6).

- paradigms: This module defines a morphological paradigm class (chapter 6).

- pynutil: This module defines the utility functions `add_weight`, `delete`, `insert`, and `join`.

- rewrite: This module defines rule application functions (section 5.3).

- rule_cascade: This module defines a rule cascade class used to apply multiple rules to a string (section 5.4).

- tagger: This module defines a tagger automaton class (subsection 5.5.3).

- utf8: This module defines functions used to generate automata matching valid UTF-8 strings encoded as byte sequences. Like the constants in byte, these can also be used to construct the Σ^* automaton used to compile rewrite rules over UTF-8-encoded bytestrings.

A P P E N D I X D

Pynini Examples Library

The Pynini package also includes a collection of example libraries reviewed in this text, distributed in the pynini.examples namespace, and associated unit tests. A brief summary of each example module is given below.

- case: This module defines a finite-state grammar for generating Finnish locative case forms (subsection 5.5.2).

- chatspeak: This module contains classes used to process "chatspeak" (section 7.4).

- chatspeak_model: This module combines the components from the previous model and uses a language model to resolve ambiguity (section 7.4).

- dates: This module defines a finite-state grammar for processing English date expressions (section 7.2).

- g2p: This module defines a finite-state grammar for Spanish grapheme-to-phoneme conversion (subsection 5.5.1).

- numbers: This module defines a finite-state grammar for processing English number names (section 7.3).

- plurals: This module defines a finite-state grammar for generating English noun plurals (subsection 5.4.3).

- t9: This module defines a class for disambiguating T9 text (section 7.5).

- weather: This module defines a finite-state grammar for generating weather expressions (section 7.6).

APPENDIX E

Pynini Export Library

The Pynini package also includes a library, distributed in the `pynini.export` namespace, that can be used to automate exporting FST grammar rules to a FAR file. Below, we provide an example of exporting FSTs `rule1` and `rule2` to a FAR file `grammar.far`.

```python
from pynini.export import export

...

exporter = export.Exporter("grammar.far")
exporter.export("rule1", rule1)
exporter.export("rule2", rule2)
exporter.close()
```

Bibliography

Cyril Allauzen and Mehryar Mohri. Efficient algorithms for testing the twins property. *Journal of Automata, Languages and Combinatorics*, 8(2):117–144, 2003. 44

Cyril Allauzen and Michael Riley. A pushdown transducer extension for the OpenFst library. In *CIAA: Proc. of the 12th International Conference on Implementation and Application of Automata*, pages 66–77, 2012. DOI: 10.1007/978-3-642-31606-7_6 15

Cyril Allauzen, Mehryar Mohri, and Brian Roark. Generalized algorithms for constructing statistical language models. In *Proc. of the 41st Annual Meeting of the Association for Computational Linguistics*, pages 40–47, 2003. DOI: 10.3115/1075096.1075102 10

Cyril Allauzen, Mehryar Mohri, Michael Riley, and Brian Roark. A generalized construction of integrated speech recognition transducers. In *IEEE International Conference on Acoustics, Speech, and Signal Processing*, pages 761–764, 2004. DOI: 10.1109/icassp.2004.1326097 47

Cyril Allauzen, Mehryar Mohri, and Brian Roark. The design principles and algorithms of a weighted grammar library. *International Journal of Foundations of Computer Science*, 16(3):403–421, 2005. DOI: 10.1142/s0129054105003066 10

Cyril Allauzen, Michael Riley, Johan Schalkwyk, Wojciech Skut, and Mehryar Mohri. Open-Fst: A general and efficient weighted finite-state transducer library. In *CIAA: Proc. of the 12th International Conference on Implementation and Application of Automata*, pages 11–23, 2007. DOI: 10.1007/978-3-540-76336-9_3 17, 29, 42, 47

Cyril Allauzen, Michael Riley, and Johan Schalkwyk. Filters for efficient composition of weighted finite-state transducers. In *CIAA: Proc. of the 15th international Conference on Implementation and Application of Automata*, pages 28–38, 2010. DOI: 10.1007/978-3-642-18098-9_4 37

Jonathan Allen, M. Sharon Hunnicut, and Dennis Klatt. *From Text to Speech; The MITalk System*. Cambridge University Press, 1987. 77

Stephen Anderson. *The Organization of Phonology*. Academic Press, 1974. 55

Evan L. Antworth. *PC-KIMMO: A Two-Level Processor for Morphological Analysis*. Summer Institute of Linguistics, 1990. DOI: 10.2307/416957 29, 80

Diana Archangeli. Underspecification in Yawelmani phonology and morphology. Ph.D. thesis, Massachusetts Institute of Technology, 1984. 88, 89

Arturo Argueta and David Chiang. Decoding with finite-state transducers on GPUs. In *Proc. of the 15th Conference of the European Chapter of the Association for Computational Linguistics: Volume 1, Long Papers*, pages 1044–1052, 2017. DOI: 10.18653/v1/e17-1098 107

Arturo Argueta and David Chiang. Composing finite state transducers on GPUs. In *Proc. of the 56th Annual Meeting of the Association for Computational Linguistics (Volume 1: Long Papers)*, pages 2697–2705, 2018. DOI: 10.18653/v1/p18-1251 107

Mark Aronoff. *Morphology by Itself.* MIT Press, 1994. DOI: 10.2307/416331 91

Mark Aronoff and Kirsten Fudemann. *What Is Morphology?*, 2nd ed., Wiley-Blackwell, 2011. 91

Philip Arthur, Graham Neubig, and Satoshi Nakamura. Incorporating discrete translation lexicons into neural machine translation. In *Proc. of the Conference on Empirical Methods in Natural Language Processing*, pages 1557–1567, 2016. DOI: 10.18653/v1/d16-1162 106

Ai Ti Aw and Lian Hau Lee. Personalized normalization for a multilingual chat system. In *Proc. of the ACL System Demonstrations*, pages 31–36, 2012. 99

Timothy Baldwin, Young-Bum Kim, Marie Catherine de Marneffe, Alan Ritter, Bo Han, and Wei Xu. Shared tasks of the 2015 Workshop on Noisy User-Generated Text: Twitter lexical normalization and named entity recognition. In *Proc. of the Workshop on Noisy User-Generated Text*, pages 126–136, 2015. DOI: 10.18653/v1/W15-4319 99

Alan Bale and Charles Reiss. *Phonology: A Formal Introduction.* MIT Press, 2018. 51, 74

Richard Beaufort, Sophie Roekhaut, Louise-Amélie Cougnon, and Cédrick Fairon. A hybrid rule/model-based finite-state framework for normalizing SMS messages. In *Proc. of the 48th Annual Meeting of the Association for Computational Linguistics*, pages 770–779, 2010. 99

Sarah Beemer, Zak Boston, April Bukoski, Daniel Chen, Princess Dickens, Andrew Gerlach, Torin Hopkins, Parth Anand Jawale, Chris Koski, Akanksha Malhotra, Piyush Mishra, Saliha Muradoglu, Lan Sang, Tyler Short, Sagarika Shreevastava, Elizabeth Spaulding, Testumichi Umada, Beilei Xiang, Changbing Yang, and Mans Hulden. Linguist vs. machine: Rapid development of finite-state morphological grammars. In *Proc. of the 17th SIG-MORPHON Workshop on Computational Research in Phonetics, Phonology, and Morphology*, pages 162–170, 2020. DOI: 10.18653/v1/2020.sigmorphon-1.18 92

Kenneth R. Beesley. Kleene, a free and open-source language for finite-state programming. In *Proc. of the 10th International Workshop on Finite State Methods and Natural Language Processing*, pages 50–54, 2012. 29

Kenneth R. Beesley and Lari Karttunen. *Finite State Morphology*. CSLI, 2003. DOI: 10.1093/oxfordhb/9780199276349.013.0018 xv, 29

Toms Bergmanis, Katharina Kann, Hinrich Schütze, and Sharon Goldwater. Training data augmentation for low-resource morphological inflection. In *Proc. of the CoNLL SIGMORPHON Shared Task: Universal Morphological Reinflection*, pages 31–39, 2017. DOI: 10.18653/v1/k17-2002 107

Juliette Blevins. A reconsideration of Yokuts vowels. *International Journal of American Linguistics*, 70(1):33–51, 2004. DOI: 10.1086/422265 88

Leonard Bloomfield. Menomini morphophonemics. *Travaux de Cercle Linguistique de Prague*, 8:105–115, 1939. 49

Hugo Braun, Justin Luitjens, Ryan Leary, Tim Kaldewey, and Daniel Povey. GPU-accelerated Viterbi exact lattice decoder for batched online and offline speech recognition. In *International Conference on Acoustics, Speech, and Signal Processing*, pages 7874–7878, 2020. DOI: 10.1109/icassp40776.2020.9054099 108

Jane Chandlee. Strictly local phonological processes. Ph.D. thesis, University of Delaware, 2014. 108

Jane Chandlee, Rémi Eyraud, and Jeffrey Heinz. Learning strictly local subsequential functions. *Transactions of the Association for Computational Linguistics*, 2:491–503, 2014. DOI: 10.1162/tacl_a_00198 108

Jane Chandlee, Rémi Eyraud, and Jeffrey Heinz. Output strictly local functions. In *Proc. of the 14th Meeting on the Mathematics of Language*, pages 112–125, 2015. DOI: 10.3115/v1/w15-2310 108

Jane Chandlee, Jeffrey Heinz, and Adam Jardine. Input strictly local opaque maps. *Phonology*, 35(2):171–205, 2018. DOI: 10.1017/s0952675718000027 56

Zhehuai Chen, Justin Luitjens, Hainan Xu, Yiming Wang, Daniel Povey, and Sanjeev Khudanpur. A GPU-based WFST decoder with exact lattice generation. In *Proc. of INTERSPEECH*, pages 2212–2216, 2018. DOI: 10.21437/interspeech.2018-1339 108

Noam Chomsky. Morphophonemics of Modern Hebrew. Master's thesis, University of Pennsylvania, 1951. DOI: 10.4324/9780203357453 49

Noam Chomsky. Formal properties of grammars. In R. Duncan Luce, Robert R. Bush, and Eugene Galanter, Eds., *Handbook of Mathematical Psychology II*, pages 323–418, John Wiley & Sons, 1963. 1, 15

Noam Chomsky and Morris Halle. *The Sound Pattern of English*. Harper and Row, 1968. DOI: 10.2307/410790 49, 80

Monojit Choudhury, Rahul Saraf, Vijit Jain, Sudesha Sarkar, and Anupam Basu. Investigation and modeling of the structure of texting language. *International Journal of Document Analysis and Recognition*, 10:157–174, 2007. DOI: 10.1007/s10032-007-0054-0 99

Grzegorz Chrupała. Normalizing tweets with edit scripts and recurrent neural embeddings. In *Proc. of the 52nd Annual Meeting of the Association for Computational Linguistics (Volume 2: Short Papers)*, pages 680–686, 2014. DOI: 10.3115/v1/p14-2111 99

Michael Collins and Terry Koo. Discriminative reranking for natural language parsing. *Computational Linguistics*, 31(1):25–70, 2005. DOI: 10.1162/0891201053630273 106

Maria Corkery, Yevgen Matusevych, and Sharon Goldwater. Are we there yet? Encoder-decoder neural networks as cognitive models of English past tense inflection. In *Proc. of the 57th Annual Meeting of the Association for Computational Linguistics*, pages 3868–3877, 2019. DOI: 10.18653/v1/p19-1376 106

Ryan Cotterell, Christo Kirov, John Sylak-Glassman, David Yarowsky, Jason Eisner, and Mans Hulden. The SIGMORPHON shared task: Morphological reinflection. In *Proc. of the 14th Annual SIGMORPHON Workshop on Computational Research in Phonetics, Phonology, and Morphology*, pages 10–22, 2016. DOI: 10.18653/v1/w16-2002 92

Ryan Cotterell, Christo Kirov, John Sylak-Glassman, Géraldine Walther, Ekaterina Vylomova, Patrick Xia, Manaal Faruqui, Sandra Kübler, and David Yarowsky. CoNLL–SIGMORPHON 2017 shared task: Universal morphological reinflection in 52 languages. In *CoNLL–SIGMORPHON Shared Task: Universal Morphological Reinflection*, pages 1–30, 2017. DOI: 10.18653/v1/K17-2001 92

Ryan Cotterell, Christo Kirov, John Sylak-Glassman, Géraldine Walther, Ekaterina Vylomova, Arya D. McCarthy, Katharina Kann, Sabrina J. Mielke, Garrett Nicolai, Miikka Silfverberg, David Yarowsky, Jason Eisner, and Mans Hulden. The CoNLL–SIGMORPHON 2018 shared task: Universal morphological reinflection. In *Proc. of the CoNLL–SIGMORPHON Shared Task: Universal Morphological Reinflection*, pages 1–27, 2018. DOI: 10.18653/v1/K18-3001 92

David Crystal. *Language and the Internet*. Cambridge University Press, 2006. DOI: 10.1017/CBO9780511487002 103

David Crystal. *Txtng: The Gr8 Db8*. Oxford University Press, 2008. 101, 103

Kees van Deemter, Emiel Krahmer, and Mariët Theune. Real vs. template-based natural language generation: A false opposition? *Computational Linguistics*, 31(1):15–24, 2005. DOI: 10.1162/0891201053630291 102

Mathieu Dehouck and Pascal Denis. A framework for understanding the role of morphology in universal dependency parsing. In *Proc. of the Conference on Empirical Methods in Natural Language Processing*, pages 2864–2870, 2018. DOI: 10.18653/v1/d18-1312 79

Arthur Dempster, Nan Laird, and Donald Rubin. Maximum likelihood from incomplete data via the EM algorithm. *Journal of the Royal Statistical Society*, 39(1):1–38, 1977. DOI: 10.1111/j.2517-6161.1977.tb01600.x 44

Pascal Denis and Benoît Sagot. Coupling an annotated corpus and a morphosyntactic lexicon for state-of-the-art POS tagging with less human effort. In *Proc. of the 23rd Pacific Asia Conference on Language, Information and Computation, Volume 1*, pages 110–119, 2009. 79

Edsger W. Dijkstra. A note on two problems in connexion with graphs. *Numerische Mathematik*, 1:269–271, 1959. DOI: 10.1007/bf01386390 46

Senka Drobac, Miikka Silfverberg, and Anssi Yli-Jyrä. Implementation of replace rules using preference operator. In *Proc. of the 10th International Workshop on Finite State Methods and Natural Language Processing*, pages 55–59, 2012. 63, 75

San Duanmu. Recursive constraint evaluation in Optimality Theory: Evidence from cyclic compounds in Shanghai. *Natural Language and Linguistic Theory*, 15(3):465–507, 1997. DOI: 10.1023/A:1005745617857 56

Amit Dubey. What to do when lexicalization fails: Parsing German with suffix analysis and smoothing. In *Proc. of the 43rd Annual Meeting of the Association for Computational Linguistics*, pages 314–321, 2005. DOI: 10.3115/1219840.1219879 79

Peter Ebden and Richard Sproat. The Kestrel TTS text normalization system. *Natural Language Engineering*, 21(3):1–21, 2014. DOI: 10.1017/s1351324914000175 73, 75, 103

Jacob Eisenstein. What to do about bad language on the internet. In *Proc. of the Conference of the North American Chapter of the Association for Computational Linguistics: Human Language Technologies*, pages 359–369, 2013. 103

Jacob Eisenstein. *Introduction to Natural Language Processing*. MIT Press, 2019. 15

Jason Eisner. Efficient generation in Primitive Optimality Theory. In *35th Annual Meeting of the Association for Computational Linguistics and 8th Conference of the European Chapter of the Association for Computational Linguistics*, pages 313–320, 1997. DOI: 10.3115/979617.979657 56

Marzieh Fadaee, Arianna Bisazza, and Christof Monz. Data augmentation for low-resource neural machine translation. In *Proc. of the 55th Annual Meeting of the Association for Computational Linguistics (Volume 2: Short Papers)*, pages 567–573, 2017. DOI: 10.18653/v1/p17-2090 107

Alexander Fraser, Helmut Schmid, Richárd Farkas, Renjing Wang, and Hinrich Schütze. Knowledge sources for constituent parsing of German, a morphologically rich and less-configurational language. *Computational Linguistics*, 39(1):57–85, 2013. DOI: 10.1162/coli_-a_00135 79

Daisuke Fukunaga, Yoshiki Tanaka, and Yuichi Kageyama. GPU-based WFST decoding with extra large language model. In *Proc. of INTERSPEECH*, pages 3815–3819, 2019. DOI: 10.21437/interspeech.2019-2101 108

Emden R. Ganser and Stephen C. North. An open graph visualization system and its applications to software engineering. *Software: Practice and Experience*, 30(11):1203–1233, 2000. DOI: 10.1002/1097-024x(200009)30:11<1203::aid-spe338>3.0.co;2-n 111

E. Mark Gold. Language identification in the limit. *Information and Control*, 10(5):447–474, 1967. DOI: 10.1016/s0019-9958(67)91165-5 108

Kyle Gorman. Pynini: A Python library for weighted finite-state grammar compilation. In *Proc. of the SIGFSM Workshop on Statistical NLP and Weighted Automata*, pages 75–80, 2016. DOI: 10.18653/v1/w16-2409 17, 29

Kyle Gorman and Richard Sproat. Minimally supervised models for number normalization. *Transactions of the Association for Computational Linguistics*, 4:507–519, 2016. DOI: 10.1162/tacl_a_00114 17, 103, 106

Kyle Gorman, Arya D. McCarthy, Ryan Cotterell, Ekaterina Vylomova, Miikka Silfverberg, and Magdalena Markowska. Weird inflects but OK: Making sense of morphological generation errors. In *Proc. of the 23rd Conference on Computational Natural Language Learning (CoNLL)*, pages 140–151, 2019. DOI: 10.18653/v1/k19-1014 106

Kyle Gorman, Lucas F. E. Ashby, Aaron Goyzueta, Arya D. McCarthy, Shijie Wu, and Daniel You. The SIGMORPHON shared task on multilingual grapheme-to-phoneme conversion. In *17th SIGMORPHON Workshop on Computational Research in Phonetics, Phonology, and Morphology*, pages 40–50, 2020. DOI: 10.18653/v1/2020.sigmorphon-1.2 17, 67

Jan Hajič. Morphological tagging: Data vs. dictionaries. In *1st Meeting of the North American Chapter of the Association for Computational Linguistics*, pages 94–101, 2000. 79

Morris Halle. On stress and accent in Indo-European. *Language*, 73(2):275–313, 1997. DOI: 10.2307/416020 84

Péter Halácsy, András Kornai, Csaba Oravecz, Viktor Trón, and Dániel Varga. Using a morphological analyzer in high precision POS tagging of Hungarian. In *Proc. of the 5th International Conference on Language Resources and Evaluation*, pages 2245–2248, 2006. 79

Jorge Hankamer. Morphological parsing and the lexicon. In William D. Marslen-Wilson, Ed., *Lexical Representation and Process*, pages 392–408, MIT Press, 1989. DOI: 10.7551/mit-press/4213.003.0018 50, 82

Bruce Hayes. A metrical theory of stress rules. Ph.D. thesis, Massachusetts Institute of Technology, 1980. 55

Jeffrey Heinz. The computational nature of phonological generalizations. In Larry M. Hyman and Frans Plank, Eds., *Phonological Typology*, pages 126–195, Mouton de Gruyter, 2018. DOI: 10.1515/9783110451931-005 75, 108

Jeffrey Heinz, Gregory M. Kobele, and Jason Riggle. Evaluating the complexity of Optimality Theory. *Linguistic Inquiry*, 40(2):277–288, 2009. DOI: 10.1162/ling.2009.40.2.277 56

Lars Hellsten, Brian Roark, Prasoon Goyal, Cyril Allauzen, Françoise Beaufays, Tom Ouyang, Michael Riley, and David Rybach. Transliterated mobile keyboard input via weighted finite-state transducers. In *Proc. of the 13th International Conference on Finite State Methods and Natural Language Processing (FSMNLP)*, pages 10–19, 2017. DOI: 10.18653/v1/w17-4002 103

Lee Hetherington. An efficient implementation of phonological rules using finite-state transducers. In *EUROSPEECH*, pages 1599–1602, 2001. 75

Charles F. Hockett. Two models of grammatical description. *Word*, 10:210–234, 1954. DOI: 10.1080/00437956.1954.11659524 80

John E. Hopcroft, Rajeev Motwani, and Jeffrey D. Ullman. *Introduction to Automata Theory, Languages, and Computation*, 3rd ed., Pearson, 2008. DOI: 10.1145/568438.568455 xv, 8, 15, 61

Mans Hulden. Foma: A finite-state compiler and library. In *Proc. of the Demonstrations Session at EACL*, pages 29–32, 2009. DOI: 10.3115/1609049.1609057 29

Mans Hulden. Rewrite rule grammars with multitape automata. *Language Modelling*, 5(1):107–130, 2017. DOI: 10.15398/jlm.v5i1.158 8

James Hurford. *The Linguistic Theory of Numerals*. Cambridge University Press, 1975. DOI: 10.2307/413066 103

William J. Idsardi. The computation of prosody. Ph.D. thesis, Massachusetts Institute of Technology, 1992. 55

Roman Jakobson. Russian conjugation. *Word*, 4(3):155–167, 1948. DOI: 10.1080/00437956.1948.11659338 49

Adam Jardine, Jane Chandlee, Rémi Eyraud, and Jeffrey Heinz. Very efficient learning of structured classes of subsequential functions from positive data. In *Proc. of the 12th International Conference on Grammatical Inference*, pages 94–108, 2014. 108

C. D. Johnson. *Formal Aspects of Phonological Description.* Mouton, 1972. DOI: 10.1515/9783110876000 49, 53, 55, 56, 108

Daniel Jurafsky and James H. Martin. *Speech and Language Processing*, 2nd ed., Pearson, 2009. 15

Ronald Kaplan. Three seductions of computational psycholinguistics. In P. Whitelock, M. Wood, H. Somers, R. Johnson, and P. Bennett, Eds., *Linguistic Theory and Computer Applications*, pages 149–188, Academic Press, 1987. 66

Ronald M. Kaplan. ACL lifetime achievement award: Computational psycholingistics. *Computational Linguistics*, 45(4):607–626, 2019. DOI: 10.1162/coli_a_00359 75

Ronald M. Kaplan and Martin Kay. Regular models of phonological rule systems. *Computational Linguistics*, 20(3):331–378, 1994. 56, 57, 75

Lauri Karttunen. The replace operator. In *33rd Annual Meeting of the Association for Computational Linguistics*, pages 16–23, 1995. DOI: 10.3115/981658.981661 56, 57

Lauri Karttunen. Directed replacement. In *34th Annual Meeting of the Association for Computational Linguistics*, pages 108–115, 1996. DOI: 10.3115/981863.981878 74

Lauri Karttunen. The proper treatment of optimality in computational phonology. In *Proc. of the International Workshop on Finite State Methods in Natural Language Processing*, pages 1–12, 1998. DOI: 10.3115/1611533.1611534 56, 66

Lauri Karttunen. Computing with realizational morphology. In Alexander Gelbukh, Ed., *Computational Linguistics and Intelligent Text Processing*, 2588:205–216, Springer, 2003. DOI: 10.1007/3-540-36456-0_20 80

Lauri Karttunen. ACL lifetime achievement award: Word play. *Computational Linguistics*, 33(4):443–467, 2007. DOI: 10.1162/coli.2007.33.4.443 75

Martin Kay. Non-concatenative finite-state morphology. In *3rd Conference of the European Chapter of the Association for Computational Linguistics*, pages 2–10, 1987. DOI: 10.3115/976858.976860 8

Martin Kay. ACL lifetime achievement award: A life of language. *Computational Linguistics*, 31(4):425–438, 2005. DOI: 10.1162/089120105775299159 75

Michael Kenstowicz and Charles Kisseberth. *Topics in Phonological Theory.* Academic Press, 1977. DOI: 10.2307/412593 55

Paul Kiparsky. Linguistic universals and language change. In Emmon Bach and Robert Harms, Eds., *Linguistic Universals and Language Change*, pages 171–201, Holt, Rinehart and Winston, 1968. 63

Paul Kiparsky. Phonological representations: Abstractness, opacity, and global rules. In Osamu Fujimura, Ed., *Three Dimensions in Linguistic Theory*, pages 57–86, TEC, 1973. 56

George Kiraz. *Computational Nonlinear Morphology: With Emphasis on Semitic Languages*. Cambridge University Press, 2001. DOI: 10.1017/cbo9780511497933 8

Dennis Klatt. Review of text-to-speech conversion for English. *Journal of the Acoustical Society of America*, 82(3):737–793, 1987. DOI: 10.1121/1.395275 77, 78

Stephen C. Kleene. Representation of events in nerve nets and finite automata. In Claude E. Shannon and J. McCarthy, Eds., *Automata Studies*, pages 3–42, Princeton University Press, 1956. DOI: 10.1515/9781400882618-002 1, 2, 7, 105, 106

Kimmo Koskenniemi. Two-level morphology: A general computational model for word-form recognition and production. Ph.D. thesis, University of Helsinki, 1983. 56, 62, 71, 75, 80

Kimmo Koskenniemi and Miikka Silfverberg. A method for compiling two-level rules with multiple contexts. In *Proc. of the 11th Meeting of the ACL Special Interest Group on Computational Morphology and Phonology*, pages 38–45, 2010. 63

Werner Kuich and Arto Salomaa. *Semirings, Automata, Languages*. Springer, 1986. DOI: 10.1007/978-3-642-69959-7 10

Mikko Kurimo, Sami Virpioja, Ville Turunen, and Krista Lagus. Morpho challenge 2005–2010: Evaluations and results. In *Proc. of the 11th Meeting of the ACL Special Interest Group on Computational Morphology and Phonology*, pages 87–95, 2010. 92

S.-Y. Kuroda. *Yawelmani Phonology*. MIT Press, 1967. 88

William Lane and Steven Bird. Bootstrapping techniques for polysynthetic morphological analysis. In *Proc. of the 58th Annual Meeting of the Association for Computational Linguistics*, pages 6652–6661, 2020. DOI: 10.18653/v1/2020.acl-main.594 107

Jackson Lee, Lucas F. E. Ashby, M. Elizabeth Garza, Yeonju Lee-Sikka, Sean Miller, Alan Wong, Arya D. McCarthy, and Kyle Gorman. Massively multilingual pronunciation mining with WikiPron. In *Proc. of the 12th International Conference on Language Resources and Evaluation*, pages 4223–4228, 2020. 17

Géraldine Legendre, Antonella Sorace, and Paul Smolensky. The Optimality Theory–Harmonic Grammar connection. In Paul Smolensky and Géraldine Legendre, Eds., *The Harmonic Mind*, pages 903–966, MIT Press, 2006. 56

Vladimir I. Levenshtein. Binary codes capable of correcting deletions, insertions, and reversals. *Soviet Physics Doklady*, 10(8):707–710, 1966. 95

Shanjian Li and Katsuhiko Momoi. A composition approach to language/encoding detection. In *19th International Unicode Conference*, page a322, 2001. 22

Zhenhao Li and Lucia Specia. Improving neural machine translation robustness via data augmentation: Beyond back-translation. In *Proc. of the 5th Workshop on Noisy User-Generated Text*, pages 328–336, 2019. DOI: 10.18653/v1/d19-5543 107

Franklin Mark Liang. Word hy-phen-a-tion by com-put-er. Ph.D. thesis, Stanford University, 1983. 77

Chu-Cheng Lin, Hao Zhu, Matthew R. Gormley, and Jason Eisner. Neural finite-state transducers: Beyond rational relations. In *Proc. of the Conference of the North American Chapter of the Association for Computational Linguistics: Human Language Technologies, Volume 1 (Long and Short Papers)*, pages 272–283, 2019. DOI: 10.18653/v1/n19-1024 107

Krister Lindén, Miikka Silfverberg, and Tommi A. Pirinen. HFST tools for morphology: An efficient open-source package for construction of morphological analyzers. In *State of the Art in Computational Morphology*, pages 28–47, Springer, 2009. DOI: 10.1007/978-3-642-04131-0_3 29

Fei Liu, Fuliang Weng, and Xiao Jiang. A broad-coverage normalization system for social media language. In *Proc. of the 50th Annual Meeting of the Association for Computational Linguistics (Volume 1: Long Papers)*, pages 1035–1044, 2012. 99

Christopher D. Manning. Last words: Computational linguistics and deep learning. *Computational Linguistics*, 41(4):701–707, 2015. DOI: doi:10.1162/COLI_a_00239 105

Igor L. Markov, Jacqueline Liu, and Adam Vagner. Regular expressions for fast-response COVID-19 text classification. *arXiv preprint arXiv:2102.09507v2*, 2021. xv

P. H. Matthews. *Inflectional Morphology: A Theoretical Study Based on Aspects of Latin Conjugation*. Cambridge University Press, 1972. 49

Arya D. McCarthy, Ekaterina Vylomova, Shijie Wu, Chaitanya Malaviya, Lawrence Wolf-Sonkin, Garrett Nicolai, Miikka Silfverberg, Sabrina J. Mielke, Jeffrey Heinz, Ryan Cotterell, and Mans Hulden. The SIGMORPHON shared task: Morphological analysis in context and cross-lingual transfer for inflection. In *Proc. of the 16th Workshop on Computational Research in Phonetics, Phonology, and Morphology*, pages 229–244, 2019. DOI: 10.18653/v1/w19-4226 92

Gretchen McCulloch. *Because Internet: Understanding the New Rules of Language*. Riverhead Books, 2019. 103

Warren S. McCulloch and Walter Pitts. A logical calculus of the ideas immanent in nervous activity. *Bulletin of Mathematical Biophysics*, 5(4):115–133, 1943. 1

M. Douglas McIlroy. Development of a spelling list. *IEEE Transactions on Communication*, 30(1):91–99, 1982. DOI: 10.1109/tcom.1982.1095395 77

Mehryar Mohri. Finite-state transducers in language and speech processing. *Computational Linguistics*, 23(2):269–311, 1997. 10, 43

Mehryar Mohri. Minimization algorithms for sequential transducers. *Journal of Automata, Languages and Combinatorics*, 234(1–2):177–201, 2000. DOI: 10.1016/s0304-3975(98)00115-7 43

Mehryar Mohri. Generic epsilon-removal and input epsilon-normalization algorithms for weighted transducers. *International Journal of Computer Science*, 13(1):129–143, 2002a. 7, 41

Mehryar Mohri. Semiring frameworks and algorithms for shortest-distance problems. *Journal of Automata, Languages and Combinatorics*, 7(3):321–350, 2002b. 47

Mehryar Mohri. Edit-distance of weighted automata: General definitions and algorithms. *International Journal of Computer Science*, 14(6):957–982, 2003. DOI: 10.1142/s0129054103002114 42, 103

Mehryar Mohri. Weighted automata algorithms. In Manfred Droste, Werner Kuich, and Heiko Vogler, Eds., *Handbook of Weighted Automata*, pages 213–254, Springer, 2009. DOI: 10.1007/978-3-642-01492-5_6 xv, 15, 42, 43, 47

Mehryar Mohri and Michael Riley. On the disambiguation of weighted automata. In *CIAA: Proc. of the 20th International Conference on Implementation and Application of Automata*, pages 263–278, 2015. DOI: 10.1007/978-3-319-22360-5_22 44

Mehryar Mohri and Richard Sproat. An efficient compiler for weighted rewrite rules. In *34th Annual Meeting of the Association for Computational Linguistics*, pages 231–238, 1996. DOI: 10.3115/981863.981894 56, 57, 58, 59, 75

Mehryar Mohri, Fernando Pereira, and Michael Riley. Weighted finite-state transducers in speech recognition. *Computer Speech and Language*, 16(1):69–88, 2002. DOI: 10.1006/csla.2001.0184 10

Steven Moran and Michael Cysouw. *The Unicode Cookbook for Linguists: Managing Writing Systems Using Orthography Profiles*. Language Science Press, 2018. DOI: 10.5281/zenodo.1296780 29

William Allan Neilson and Thomas A. Knott, Eds. *Webster's New International Dictionary of the English Language*, 2nd ed., C. & C. Merriam Company, 1934. DOI: 10.2307/451735 77

Stanley Newman. *Yokuts Language of California*. Viking Fund Publications in Anthropology, 1944. DOI: 10.2307/409890 88, 89

Tom Ouyang, David Rybach, Françoise Beaufays, and Michael Riley. Mobile keyboard input decoding with finite-state transducers. *arXiv Preprint arXiv:1704.03987*, 2017. 103

Barbara H. Partee, Alice ter Meulen, and Robert E. Wall. *Mathematical Methods in Linguistics*. Kluwer, 1993. DOI: 10.1007/978-94-009-2213-6 15

Gerald Penn and Paul Kiparsky. On Panini and the generative capacity of contextualized replacement systems. In *Proc. of COLING: Posters*, pages 943–950, 2012. 49

Glyne L. Piggott. More on the application of phonological rules. *Recherces linguistiques à Montréal/Montreal Working Papers in Linguistics*, 5:113–150, 1975. 55

Steven Pinker and Alan Prince. On language and connectionism: Analysis of a parallel distributed processing model of language acquisition. In Steven Pinker and Jacques Mehler, Eds., *Connections and Symbols*, MIT Press, 1988. DOI: 10.1016/0010-0277(88)90032-7 106

Martin F. Porter. An algorithm for suffix stripping. *Program*, 14(3):130–137, 1980. DOI: 10.1108/eb046814 77

R. J. D. Power and H. C. Longuet-Higgins. Learning to count: A computational model of language acquisition. *Proc. of the Royal Society*, 200:391–417, 1978. DOI: 10.1098/rspb.1978.0024 103

Alan Prince and Paul Smolensky. *Optimality Theory: Constraint Interaction in Generative Grammar*. MIT Press, 2004. DOI: 10.1002/9780470756171.ch1 56

Ernest Pusateri, Bharat Ram Ambati, Elizabeth Brooks, Ondrej Platek, Donald McAllaster, and Venki Nagesha. A mostly data-driven approach to inverse text normalization. In *Proc. of INTERSPEECH*, pages 2784–2788, 2017. DOI: 10.21437/interspeech.2017-1274 73, 105

Teresita V. Ramos and Maria Lourdes S. Bautista. *Handbook of Tagalog Verbs: Inflections, Modes, and Aspects*. University of Hawaii Press, 1986. 87

Pushpendre Rastogi, Ryan Cotterell, and Jason Eisner. Weighting finite-state transductions with neural context. In *Proc. of the Conference of the North American Chapter of the Association for Computational Linguistics: Human Language Technologies*, pages 623–633, 2016. DOI: 10.18653/v1/n16-1076 107

Dominique Revuz. Minimisation of acyclic deterministic automata in linear time. *Theoretical Computer Science*, 92(1):181–189, 1992. DOI: 10.1016/0304-3975(92)90142-3 43

Catherine O. Ringen and Orvokki Heinämäki. Variation in Finnish vowel harmony: An OT account. *Natural Language and Linguistic Theory*, 17(2):303–337, 1999. 71

Eric Sven Ristad and Peter N. Yianilos. Learning string-edit distance. *IEEE Transactions on Pattern Analysis and Machine Intelligence*, 20(5):522–532, 1998. DOI: 10.1109/34.682181 103

Sandy Ritchie, Richard Sproat, Kyle Gorman, Daan van Esch, Christian Schallhart, Bampounis Nikos, Benoît Brard, Jonas Fromseier Mortensen, Millie Holt, and Eoin Mahon. Unified verbalization for speech recognition and synthesis across languages. In *Proc. of INTERSPEECH*, pages 3530–3534, 2019. 17, 103

Brian Roark and Richard Sproat. *Computational Approaches to Morphology and Syntax*. Oxford University Press, 2007. 15, 63, 75, 80, 82, 92

Brian Roark and Richard Sproat. Hippocratic abbreviation expansion. In *Proc. of the 52nd Annual Meeting of the Association for Computational Linguistics (Volume 2: Short Papers)*, pages 364–369, 2014. DOI: 10.3115/v1/p14-2060 99

Brian Roark, Richard Sproat, Cyril Allauzen, Michael Riley, Jeffrey Sorensen, and Terry Tai. The OpenGrm open-source finite-state grammar software libraries. In *Proc. of the ACL System Demonstrations*, pages 61–66, 2012. 10, 29, 99

Emmanuel Roche and Yves Schabes. Deterministic part-of-speech tagging with finite-state transducers. *Computational Linguistics*, 21(2):227–253, 1995. 10

Henry Rogers. *Writing Systems: A Linguistic Approach*. Blackwell, 2005. 67, 79

David Rumelhart and Jay McClelland. On learning the past tenses of English verbs. In Jay Mc-Clelland, David Rumelhart, and the PDP Research Group, Eds., *Parallel Distributed Processing: Explorations into the Microstructure of Cognition. Vol. 2: Psychological and Biological Models*, pages 216–271, Bradford Books, 1986. 106

David Rybach, Michael Riley, and Johan Schalkwyk. On lattice generation for large vocabulary speech recognition. In *IEEE Automatic Speech Recognition and Understanding Workshop (ASRU)*, pages 228–235, 2017. DOI: 10.1109/asru.2017.8268940 61

Klaus U. Schulz and Stoyan Mihov. Fast string correction with Levenshtein automata. *International Journal of Document Analysis and Recognition*, 5(1):67–85, 2002. DOI: 10.1007/s10032-002-0082-8 95, 96

Lane Schwartz, Emily Chen, Benjamin Hunt, and Sylvia L. R. Schreiner. Bootstrapping a neural morphological analyzer for St. Lawrence Island Yupik from a finite-state transducer. In *Proc. of the 3rd Workshop on the Use of Computational Methods in the Study of Endangered Languages Volume 1 (Papers)*, pages 87–96, 2019. DOI: 10.33011/computel.v1i.4277 107

Libin Shen and Aravind K. Joshi. Ranking and reranking with perceptron. *Machine Learning*, 60(1–3):73–96, 2005. DOI: 10.1007/s10994-005-0918-9 106

Stuart Shieber. Evidence against the context-freeness of natural language. *Linguistics and Philosophy*, 8(3):333–343, 1985. DOI: 10.1007/bf00630917 49

Maria Shugrina. Formatting time-aligned ASR transcripts for readability. In *Human Language Technologies: The Annual Conference of the North American Chapter of the Association for Computational Linguistics*, pages 198–206, 2010. 73

Miikka Silfverberg, Adam Wiemerslage, Ling Liu, and Lingshuang Jack Mao. Data augmentation for morphological reinflection. In *Proc. of the CoNLL SIGMORPHON Shared Task: Universal Morphological Reinflection*, pages 90–99, 2017. DOI: 10.18653/v1/k17-2010 107

Wojciech Skut, Stefan Ulrich, and Kathrine Hammervold. A generic finite-state compiler for tagging rules. *Machine Translation*, 18(3):239–250, 2003. DOI: 10.1007/s10590-004-2479-2 75

Richard Sproat. *Morphology and Computation*. MIT Press, 1992. DOI: 10.7551/mit-press/4775.001.0001 91, 106

Richard Sproat. Multilingual text analysis for text-to-speech synthesis. *Natural Language Engineering*, 2(4):369–380, 1996. DOI: 10.1017/s1351324997001654 73, 98

Richard Sproat. *A Computational Theory of Writing Systems*. Cambridge University Press, 2000. DOI: 10.1162/coli.2000.27.3.464 75

Richard Sproat. *Language, Technology, and Society*. Oxford University Press, 2010a. xv

Richard Sproat. Lightly supervised learning of text normalization: Russian number names. In *IEEE Workshop on Speech and Language Technology*, pages 436–441, 2010b. DOI: 10.1109/slt.2010.5700892 98

Richard Sproat and Navdeep Jaitly. An RNN model of text normalization. In *INTERSPEECH*, pages 754–758, 2017. DOI: 10.21437/interspeech.2017-35 106, 107

Richard Sproat, Alan W. Black, Stanley Chen, Shankar Kumar, Mari Ostendorf, and Christopher Richards. Normalization of non-standard words. *Computer Speech and Language*, 15(3):287–333, 2001. DOI: 10.1006/csla.2001.0169 73

Donca Steriade. Glides and vowels in Romanian. In *Proc. of the 10th annual meeting of the Berkeley Linguistics Society*, pages 47–64, 1984. DOI: 10.3765/bls.v10i0.1935 53

Gregory T. Stump. *Inflectional Morphology: A Theory of Paradigm Structure*. Cambridge University Press, 2001. DOI: 10.1017/cbo9780511486333 80

Paul Taylor.   *Text-to-Speech Synthesis.*   Cambridge University Press, 2009. DOI: 10.1017/cbo9780511816338 73

Ken Thompson. Programming techniques: Regular expression search algorithm. *Communications of the ACM*, 11(6):419–422, 1968. DOI: 10.1145/363347.363387 41

Axel Thue. Probleme über veränderungen von zeichenreihen nach gegebenen regeln. *Skrifter Udgivne Af Videnskabs-Selskabs I. Christiana*, 10, 1914. 1

Alan Turing. On computable numbers, with an application to the Entscheidungsproblem. *Proc. of the London Mathematical Society, Series 2*, 42(1):230–265, 1936. 1

Ekaterina Vylomova, Jennifer White, Elizabeth Salesky, Sabrina J. Mielke, Shijie Wu, Edoardo Maria Ponti, Rowan Hall Maudslay, Ran Zmigrod, Josef Valvoda, Svetlana Toldova, Francis Tyers, Elena Klyachko, Ilya Yegorov, Natalia Krizhanovsky, Paula Czarnowska, Irene Nikkarinen, Andrew Krizhanovsky, Tiago Pimentel, Lucas Torroba Hennigen, Christo Kirov, Garrett Nicolai, Adina Williams, Antonios Anastasopoulos, Hilaria Cruz, Eleanor Chodroff, Ryan Cotterell, Miikka Silfverberg, and Mans Hulden. SIGMORPHON 2020 shared task 0: Typologically diverse morphological inflection. In *Proc. of the 17th SIGMORPHON Workshop on Computational Research in Phonetics, Phonology, and Morphology*, pages 1–39, 2020. 92

Robert A. Wagner and Michael J. Fischer. The string-to-string correction problem. *Journal of the Association for Computation Machinery*, 2(1):168–173, 1974. DOI: 10.1145/321796.321811 95

William F. Weigel. *Yowlumne in the 20th century*. Ph.D. thesis, University of California, Berkeley, 2005. 88

Gail Weiss, Yoav Goldberg, and Eran Yahav. Extracting automata from recurrent neural networks using queries and counterexamples. In *Proc. of the 35th International Conference on Machine Learning*, pages 5247–5256, 2018. 106

David H. Wolpert. Stacked generalization. *Neural Networks*, 5(2):241–259, 1992. DOI: 10.1016/s0893-6080(05)80023-1 106

Ke Wu, Cyril Allauzen, Keith Hall, Michael Riley, and Brian Roark. Encoding linear models as weighted finite-state transducers. In *Proc. of INTERSPEECH*, pages 1258–1262, 2014. 10

Yi Yang and Jacob Eisenstein. A log-linear model for unsupervised text normalization. In *Proc. of the Conference on Empirical Methods in Natural Language Processing*, pages 61–72, 2013. 99

David Yarowsky. Homograph disambiguation in text-to-speech synthesis. In Jan P. H. van Santen, Richard W. Sproat, Joseph P. Olive, and Julia Hirschberg, Eds., *Progress in Speech Synthesis*, pages 157–172, Springer, 1997. DOI: 10.1007/978-1-4612-1894-4_12 97

Anssi Yli-Jyrä. Transducers from parallel replace rules and modes with generalized lenient composition. In *Finite State Methods in Natural Language Processing*, pages 197–212, 2007. 75

Anssi Yli-Jyrä. On finite-state tonology with autosegmental representations. In *Proc. of the 11th International Conference on Finite State Methods and Natural Language Processing*, pages 90–98, 2013. 63, 75

Anssi Yli-Jyrä and Kimmo Koskenniemi. Compiling generalized two-level rules and grammars. In Tapio Salakoski, Filip Ginter, Sampo Pyysalo, and Tapio Pahikkala, Eds., *Advances in Natural Language Processing*, pages 174–185, Springer, 2006. DOI: 10.1007/11816508_19 63, 75

Hao Zhang, Richard Sproat, Axel H. Ng, Felix Stahlberg, Xiaochang Peng, Kyle Gorman, and Brian Roark. Neural models of text normalization for speech applications. *Computational Linguistics*, 45(2):293–337, 2019. DOI: 10.1162/coli_a_00349 73, 105, 106, 107

Arnold M. Zwicky. Topics in Sanskrit phonology. Ph.D. thesis, Massachusetts Institute of Technology, 1965. 55

Authors' Biographies

KYLE GORMAN

Kyle Gorman is an assistant professor of linguistics at the Graduate Center, City University of New York, where he directs the master's program in computational linguistics; he also works as a software engineer at Google. He was previously an assistant professor at the Oregon Health & Science University in Portland. He holds a Ph.D. in linguistics from the University of Pennsylvania. His research interests include phonology, morphology, and speech and text processing. He is a maintainer of the OpenFst and OpenGrm libraries and the creator of Pynini. He lives in Brooklyn.

RICHARD SPROAT

Richard Sproat received his Ph.D. in linguistics from the Massachusetts Institute of Technology in 1985. Since then, he has worked in a number of areas of linguistics and computational linguistics, but he is perhaps best known for his work on text normalization for speech applications such as text-to-speech synthesis. His recent interests include neural text processing, finite-state methods, and computational models of writing systems. He is currently a research scientist at Google in Tokyo.

Index

Printed in the United States
by Baker & Taylor Publisher Services